PRAISE FOR *TRIGGERS*

"*Triggers* can give you the self-awareness you need—to create your own world—rather than being created by the world around you." Alan Mulally, US CEO of the Year (CEO magazine) and #3 Greatest Leader in the World (*Fortune* magazine).

PRAISE FOR MARSHALL GOLDSMITH

"The number seven greatest business thinker in the world" *Harvard Business Review*

"One of the most credible thought leaders in the new era of business" *The Economist*

"An influential practitioner in the history of leadership development" *Businessweek*

"A top executive educator" *Wall Street Journal*

"One of the five most-respected executive coaches in the world" *Forbes*

"A great communicator" *O (Oprah Magazine)*

MARSHALL GOLDSMITH is corporate America's preeminent executive coach. He is one of a select few consultants who have been asked to work with more than eighty CEOs in the world's top corporations. He has helped implement leadership development processes that have impacted more than one million people. His PhD is from UCLA and he is on the faculty of the executive education programs at Dartmouth College's Tuck School of Business. The American Management Association recently named Marshall one of fifty great thinkers and business leaders who have impacted the field of management, and *Businessweek* listed him as one of the most influential practitioners in the history of leadership development. In 2006, Alliant International University renamed their schools of business and organisational psychology The Marshall Goldsmith School of Management.

MARK REITER has collaborated on thirteen previous books. He is also a literary agent in Bronxville, New York.

Triggers

ALSO BY MARSHALL GOLDSMITH WITH MARK REITER

What Got You Here Won't Get You There

Mojo

Triggers

Sparking Positive Change

and Making it Last

Marshall Goldsmith
and Mark Reiter

P

PROFILE BOOKS

First published in Great Britain in 2015 by
PROFILE BOOKS LTD
3 Holford Yard
Bevin Way
London
WC1X 9HD
www.profilebooks.com

Copyright © Marshall Goldsmith, Inc, 2015

First published in the United States of America by Crown Business, an
imprint of Random House, Inc., New York, 2015

Printed and bound in India by
Manipal Technologies Ltd, Manipal

The moral right of the author has been asserted.

Illustrations by Nigel Holmes

A CIP catalogue record for this book is available from the British
Library.

ISBN 978 1 78125 281 9
eISBN 978 1 78283 079 5

Triggers is dedicated to my two wonderful grandchildren, Avery Reid Shriner and Austin Marshall Shriner.

I saw a beggar leaning on his wooden crutch,
He said to me, "You must not ask for so much."
And a pretty woman leaning in her darkened door,
She cried to me, "Hey, why not ask for more?"

—*Leonard Cohen, "Bird on a Wire"*

Contents

Introduction   xiii

PART ONE

Why Don't We Become the Person We Want to Be?

Chapter 1:   The Immutable Truths of Behavioral Change   3

Chapter 2:   Belief Triggers That Stop Behavioral Change in Its Tracks   12

Chapter 3:   It's the Environment   25

Chapter 4:   Identifying Our Triggers   39

Chapter 5:   How Triggers Work   54

Chapter 6:   We Are Superior Planners and Inferior Doers   62

Chapter 7:   Forecasting the Environment   73

Chapter 8:   The Wheel of Change   84

PART TWO

Try

Chapter 9:   The Power of Active Questions   101

Chapter 10:   The Engaging Questions   111

Chapter 11:   Daily Questions in Action   124

Chapter 12:   Planner, Doer, *and* Coach   140

Chapter 13:   AIWATT   152

PART THREE

More Structure, Please

Chapter 14: We Do Not Get Better Without Structure   169

Chapter 15: But It Has to Be the Right Structure   175

Chapter 16: Behaving Under the Influence of Depletion   181

Chapter 17: We Need Help When We're Least Likely to Get
It   189

Chapter 18: Hourly Questions   194

Chapter 19: The Trouble with "Good Enough"   202

Chapter 20: Becoming the Trigger   216

PART FOUR

No Regrets

Chapter 21: The Circle of Engagement   221

Chapter 22: The Hazard of Leading a Changeless Life   232

Acknowledgments   235
Index   236

My colleague Phil tripped down his basement steps and landed hard on his head. For a few moments as he lay on the floor, his arms and shoulders tingling, he thought he was paralyzed. Too wobbly to stand up, he sat against a wall and assessed the damage. The tingling in his limbs meant he still retained feeling (a good thing). His head and neck were throbbing. He could feel blood trickling down his back from a lacerated scalp. He knew that he needed to go to an ER so they could clean up the wound and check for broken bones and internal bleeding. He also knew he was in no shape to drive himself.

It was a Saturday morning. Phil's wife and grown sons were not home. He was alone in his quiet suburban house. He pulled his cell phone out to call for help. As he scrolled through names he realized he didn't have a single friend nearby whom he felt comfortable calling in an emergency. He'd never made the effort to know his neighbors. Reluctant to call 911 since he wasn't gushing blood or having a heart attack, Phil tracked down the home number of a middle-aged couple a few houses away and dialed. A woman named Kay answered, someone he acknowledged on the street but had rarely spoken to. He explained his situation and Kay rushed over, entering Phil's home through an unlocked back door. She found Phil in the basement, helped him to his feet, and drove him to the local hospital, staying with him during the five hours he was examined. Yes, he'd suffered a concussion, the doctors said, and he'd be in pain for a few weeks, but nothing was broken and he'd recover. Kay drove him back to his house.

Resting in his dark house later that day, Phil thought about how close he had come to disaster. He recalled the moment when his head hit the concrete floor, the bright brittle sound at impact, like a hammer coming down on a marble counter and shattering the stone into tiny pieces. He remembered the electrical charge coursing through his limbs and the terror he felt at the prospect of never walking again. He thought about how lucky he was.

But Phil's fall triggered more than gratitude for not being crippled. He also reflected on the remarkable kindness of his neighbor Kay, and how she had selflessly given up her day for him. For the first time in years, he thought about how he was living his life. Phil told himself, "I need to get better at making friends." Not because he might need people like Kay to save him in the future, but because he wanted to become more like Kay.

Not all of us require a violent life-threatening knock on the head to change our behavior. It only seems that way.

| | |

This is a book about adult behavioral change. Why are we so bad at it? How do we get better at it? How do we choose what to change? How do we make others appreciate that we've changed? How can we strengthen our resolve to wrestle with the timeless, omnipresent challenge any successful person must stare down—becoming the person we want to be?

To answer these questions, I'll begin by focusing on the triggers in our environment. Their impact is profound.

A trigger is any stimulus that reshapes our thoughts and actions. In every waking hour we are being triggered by people, events, and circumstances that have the potential to change us. These triggers appear suddenly and unexpectedly. They can be major moments, like Phil's concussion, or as minor as a paper cut. They can be pleasant, like a teacher's praise that elevates our discipline and ambition—and turns our life around 180 degrees. Or they can be counterproductive, like an ice-cream cone that tempts us off our diet or peer pressure that confuses us into doing something we know is wrong. They can stir our competitive instincts, from the common workplace carrot of a bigger paycheck to the annoying sight of a rival outdistancing us. They can drain us, like the news that a loved one is seriously ill or that our company is up for sale. They can be as elemental as the sound of rain triggering a sweet memory.

Triggers are practically infinite in number. Where do they come from? Why do they make us behave against our interests? Why are we oblivious to them? How do we pinpoint the triggering moments that anger us, or throw us off course, or make us feel that all is right in the world—so we can avoid the bad ones, repeat the good ones? How do we make triggers work for us?

Our environment is the most potent triggering mechanism in our lives—and not always for our benefit. We make plans, set goals, and stake our happiness on achieving these goals. But our environment constantly intervenes. The smell of bacon wafts up from the kitchen, and we forget our doctor's advice about lowering our cholesterol. Our colleagues work late every night, so we feel obliged to match their commitment, and miss one of our kid's baseball games, then another, then another. Our phone chirps, and we glance at the glowing screen instead of looking into the eyes of the person we love. This is how our environment triggers undesirable behavior.

Because our environmental factors are so often outside of our control, we may think there is not much we can do about them. We feel like victims of circumstance. Puppets of fate. I don't accept that. Fate is the hand of cards we've been dealt. Choice is how we play the hand.

Despite a hard knock on the head, Phil didn't bend to circumstance. His *fate* was to fall, hit his head, and recover. His *choice* was to become a better neighbor.

| | |

There's an emotion we're all familiar with hovering over these pages rather than coursing through them. It's not explicit. But that doesn't mean it's less real. It's the feeling of *regret*. It's implied every time we ask ourselves why we haven't become the person we want to be.

A big part of my research for this book involved asking people the simple question, "What's the biggest behavioral change you've ever made?" The answers run the gamut, but the most poignant ones—guaranteed to raise the emotional temperature in the room—come from people recalling the behavior they should have changed but didn't. They're reflecting on their failure to become the person they wanted to be. And it often overwhelms them with desolate feelings of regret.

We are not like Jane Austen's overbearing Lady Catherine de Bourgh (from *Pride and Prejudice*), who boasts of her natural taste in music, then without a sixteenth note of irony, says, "If I had ever learnt, I should have been a great proficient." Unlike Lady Catherine, we feel regret's sharp sting when we reflect on the opportunities squandered, the choices deferred, the efforts not made, the talents never developed in our lives. Usually when it's too late to do much about it.

Regret was definitely in the air when I interviewed Tim, a once-powerful executive producer of a network sports division. Tim's network career ended prematurely when he was in his mid-forties because he didn't get along with his superiors. A decade later, in his mid-fifties, Tim was getting by with consulting jobs. He still had an expertise that companies needed. But he would never find the stable executive position he once had. He has a reputation: *doesn't play well with others.*

Tim has had years to confront the reasons for this reputation. But he never articulated them until the day his daughter asked for fatherly advice before she started her first TV job.

"I told her the greatest virtue is patience," Tim said. "You're operating in a business where everyone's looking at the clock. A show starts and ends precisely at a given time. The control booth screens display everything in hundredths of a second. And it never stops. There's always another show to do. The clock is always ticking. This creates an incredible sense of urgency in everyone. But if you're in charge, it also tests your patience. You want everything done *now*, or even sooner. You become very demanding, and when you don't get what you want, you can get frustrated and angry. You start treating people as the enemy. They're not only disappointing you but making you look bad. And then you get angry."

That was a triggering moment for Tim. Until he said it he hadn't realized how much his professional impatience was influenced by a savage network TV environment—and how it had seeped into other parts of his life.

He explained: "I saw that I'm the kind of guy who emails a friend and gets mad if I don't hear back within the hour. Then I start harassing that friend for ignoring me. Basically, I'm treating my friends the way I used to treat production assistants. It's how I face the world. That's no way to live."

Tim needed an intimate father-daughter encounter to trigger an insight that fed the powerful feeling of regret. "If I could change anything about my life," he concluded, "I'd be more patient."

Regret is the emotion we experience when we assess our present circumstances and reconsider how we got here. We replay what we actually did against what we should have done—and find ourselves wanting in some way. Regret can hurt.

For such a penetrating and wounding emotion, regret doesn't get much respect. We treat it as a benign factor, something to deny or rationalize away. We tell ourselves, "I've made stupid choices but they've made me who I am today. Lamenting the past is a waste of time. I learned my lesson. Let's move on." That's one way of looking at regret—if only as a form of self-protection from the pain of knowing we missed out. We're comforted by the fact that no one is immune to regret (we're not alone) and that time heals all wounds (the only thing worse than experiencing pain is not knowing if and when the pain will go away).

I want to suggest a different attitude, namely embracing regret (although not too tightly or for too long). The pain that comes with regret should be mandatory, not something to be shooed away like an annoying pet. When we make bad choices and fail ourselves or hurt the people we love, we *should* feel pain. That pain can be motivating and in the best sense, triggering—a reminder that maybe we messed up but we can do better. It's one of the most powerful feelings guiding us to change.

If I do my job properly here and you do your part, two things will happen: 1) you will move closer to becoming the person you want to be and 2) you'll have less regret.

Shall we get started?

Part One

Why Don't We Become the Person We Want to Be?

Chapter 1

The Immutable Truths
of Behavioral Change

As an executive coach, I've been helping successful leaders achieve positive lasting change in behavior for more than thirty-five years. While almost all of my clients embrace the opportunity to change, some are a little reluctant in the beginning. Most are aware of the fact that behavioral change will help them become more effective leaders, partners, and even family members. A few are not.

My process of helping clients is straightforward and consistent. I interview and listen to my clients' key stakeholders. These stakeholders could be their colleagues, direct reports, or board members. I accumulate a lot of confidential feedback. Then I go over the summary of this feedback with my clients. My clients take ultimate responsibility for the behavioral changes that they want to make. My job is then very simple. I help my clients achieve positive, lasting change in the behavior that *they* choose as judged by key stakeholders that *they* choose. If my clients succeed in achieving this positive change—as judged by their stakeholders—I get paid. If the key stakeholders do not see positive change, I don't get paid.

Our odds of success improve because I'm with the client every step of the way, telling him or her how to stay on track and not regress to a former self. But that doesn't diminish the importance of these two immutable truths:

Truth #1: Meaningful behavioral change is very hard to do.

It's hard to initiate behavioral change, even harder to stay the course, hardest of all to make the change stick. I'd go so far as to say that adult behavioral change is the most difficult thing for sentient human beings to accomplish.

If you think I'm overstating its difficulty, answer these questions:

- *What do you want to change in your life?* It could be something major, such as your weight (a big one), your job (big too), or your career (even bigger). It could be something minor, such as changing your hairstyle or checking in with your mother more often or changing the wall color in your living room. It's not my place to judge what you want to change.
- *How long has this been going on?* For how many months or years have you risen in the morning and told yourself some variation on the phrase, "This is the day I make a change"?
- *How's that working out?* In other words, can you point

to a specific moment when you decided to change
something in your life and you acted on the impulse
and it worked out to your satisfaction?

The three questions conform to the three problems we face
in introducing change into our lives.

We can't admit that we need to change—either because we're
unaware that a change is desirable, or more likely, we're aware
but have reasoned our way into elaborate excuses that deny
our need for change. In the following pages, we'll examine—
and dispense with—the deep-seated beliefs that trigger our
resistance to change.

We do not appreciate inertia's power over us. Given the
choice, we prefer to do nothing—which is why I suspect our
answers to "How long has this been going on?" are couched
in terms of years rather than days. Inertia is the reason we
never start the process of change. It takes extraordinary effort to *stop* doing something in our comfort zone (because
it's painless or familiar or mildly pleasurable) in order to *start*
something difficult that will be good for us in the long run. I
cannot supply the required effort in this book. That's up to
you. But through a simple process emphasizing structure and
self-monitoring I can provide you with the kick start that triggers and sustains positive change.

We don't know how to execute a change. There's a difference
between motivation and understanding and ability. For example, we may be *motivated* to lose weight but we lack the nutri-
tional *understanding* and cooking *ability* to design and stick
with an effective diet. Or flip it over: we have understanding
and ability but lack the motivation. One of the central tenets
of this book is that our behavior is shaped, both positively

and negatively, by our environment—and that a keen appreciation of our environment can dramatically lift not only our motivation, ability, and understanding of the change process, but also our confidence that we can actually do it.

I vividly recall my first decisive behavioral change as an adult. I was twenty-six years old, married to my first and only wife, Lyda, and pursuing a doctorate in organizational behavior at the University of California, Los Angeles. Since high school I had been a follicly challenged man, but back then I was loath to admit it. Each morning I would spend several minutes in front of the bathroom mirror carefully arranging the wispy blond stands of hair still remaining on the top of my head. I'd smooth the hairs forward from back to front, then curve them to a point in the middle of my forehead, forming a pattern that looked vaguely like a laurel wreath. Then I'd walk out into the world with my ridiculous comb-over, convinced I looked normal like everyone else.

When I visited my barber, I'd give specific instructions on how to cut my hair. One morning I dozed off in the chair, so he trimmed my hair too short, leaving insufficient foliage on the sides to execute my comb-over regimen. I could have panicked and put on a hat for a few weeks, waiting for the strands to grow back. But as I stood in front of the mirror later that day, staring at my reflected image, I said to myself, "Face it, you're bald. It's time you accepted it."

That's the moment when I decided to shave the few remaining hairs on the top of my head and live my life as a bald man. It wasn't a complicated decision and it didn't take great effort to accomplish. A short trim at the barber from then on. But in many ways, it is still the most liberating change

I've made as an adult. It made me happy, at peace with my appearance.

I'm not sure what triggered my acceptance of a new way of self-grooming. Perhaps I was horrified at the prospect of starting every day with this routine forever. Or maybe it was the realization that I wasn't fooling anyone.

The reason doesn't matter. The real achievement is that I actually decided to change and successfully acted on that decision. That's not easy to do. I had spent years fretting and fussing with my hair. That's a long time to continue doing something that I knew, on the spectrum of human folly, fell somewhere between vain and idiotic. And yet I persisted in this foolish behavior for so many years because (a) I couldn't admit that I was bald, and (b) under the sway of inertia, I found it easier to continue doing my familiar routine than change my ways. The one advantage I had was (c) I knew how to execute the change. Unlike most changes—for example, getting in shape, learning a new language, or becoming a better listener—it didn't require months of discipline and measuring and following up. Nor did it require the cooperation of others. I just needed to stop giving my barber crazy instructions and let him do his job. If only all our behavioral changes were so uncomplicated.

Truth #2: No one can make us change
unless we truly want to change.

This should be self-evident. Change has to come from within. It can't be dictated, demanded, or otherwise forced upon people. A man or woman who does not wholeheartedly commit to change will never change.

I didn't absorb this simple truth until my twelfth year in the "change" business. By then I had done intensive one-on-one coaching with more than a hundred executives, nearly all successes but a smattering of failures, too.

As I reviewed my failures, one conclusion leapt out: *Some people say they want to change, but they don't really mean it.* I had erred profoundly in client selection. I believed the clients when they said they were committed to changing, but I had not drilled deeper to determine if they were telling the truth.

Not long after this revelation, I was asked to work with Harry, the chief operating officer of a large consulting firm. Harry was a smart, motivated, hardworking deliver-the-numbers alpha male who was also arrogant and overdelighted with himself. He was habitually disrespectful to his direct reports, driving several of them away to work for the competition. This development rattled the CEO, hence the call to me to coach Harry.

Harry talked a good game at first, assuring me that he was eager to get started and get better. I interviewed his colleagues and direct reports, even his wife and teenage children. They all told the same story. Despite his abundant professional qualities, Harry had an overwhelming need to be the smartest person in the room, always proving that he was right, winning every argument. It was exhausting and off-putting. Who could say how many opportunities had vanished because people loathed being pummeled and browbeaten?

As Harry and I reviewed his 360-degree feedback, he claimed to value the opinions of his co-workers and family members. Yet whenever I brought up an area for improvement, Harry would explain point by point how his questionable behavior was actually justified. He'd remind me that he majored in psychology in college and then analyze the behavioral problems of everyone around him, concluding that *they* needed to change. In a mind-bending display of chutzpah, he asked me for suggestions in helping these people get better.

In my younger days, I would have overlooked Harry's resistance. Mimicking his arrogance and denial, I would have convinced myself that I could help Harry where lesser mortals would fail. Fortunately I remembered my earlier lesson: *Some people say they want to change, but they don't really mean it.* It was dawning on me that Harry was using our work together as another opportunity to display his superiority and to reverse the misperceptions of all the confused people surrounding him, including his wife and kids. By our fourth meeting I gave up the ghost. I told Harry that my coaching wouldn't be helpful to him and we parted ways. (I felt neither joy nor surprise when I later learned that the firm had fired Harry. Evidently the CEO had concluded that an individual who actively resists help has maxed out professionally and personally.)

I often call up my time with Harry as a stark example that, even when altering our behavior represents all reward and no risk—and clinging to the status quo can cost us our careers and relationships—we resist change.

We're even defeated by change when it's a matter of life and death. Consider how hard it is to break a bad habit such as smoking. It's so daunting that, despite the threat of cancer and widespread social disapproval, two-thirds of smokers who say they'd like to quit never even try. And of those who do try, nine out of ten fail. And of those who eventually quit—

namely the most motivated and disciplined people—on average they fail six times before succeeding.

Compared to other behavioral changes in our lives, smoking is a relatively simple challenge. After all, it's a self-contained behavior. It's just you and your habit, a lone individual dealing with one demon. You either lick it or you don't. It's up to you—and only you—to declare victory. No one else gets a say in the matter.

Imagine how much harder it is when you let other people into the process—people whose actions are unpredictable, beyond your control—and their responses can affect your success. It's the difference between hitting warm-up tennis balls over the net and playing a match where an opponent is rocketing the balls back at you.

That's what makes adult behavioral change so hard. If you want to be a better partner at home or a better manager at work, you not only have to change your ways, you have to get some buy-in from your partner or co-workers. Everyone around you has to recognize that you're changing. Relying on other people increases the degree of difficulty exponentially.

Let that last sentence sink in before you turn the page. This is not a book about stopping a bad habit such as smoking cigarettes or dealing with your late-night craving for ice cream. Nicotine and ice cream aren't the target constituency here. It's about changing your behavior when you're among people you respect and love. They are your target audience.

What makes positive, lasting behavioral change so challenging—and causes most of us to give up early in the game—is that we have to do it in our imperfect world, full of triggers that may pull and push us off course.

The good news is that behavioral change does not have to

be complicated. As you absorb the methods in the following pages, do not be lulled into dismissiveness because my advice sounds simple. Achieving meaningful and lasting change may be simple—simpler than we imagine.

But *simple* is far from *easy*.

Chapter 2

Belief Triggers That Stop Behavioral Change in Its Tracks

During the twelve years he was mayor of New York City, from 2001 to 2013, Michael Bloomberg was an indefatigable "social engineer," always striving to change people's behavior for the better (at least in his mind). Whether he was banning public smoking or decreeing that all municipal vehicles go hybrid, his objective was always civic self-improvement. Near the end of his third and final term in 2012, he decided to attack the childhood obesity epidemic. He did so by banning sales of sugary soft drinks in quantities greater than sixteen ounces. We can debate the merits of Bloomberg's idea and the inequities created by some of its loopholes. But we can all agree that reducing childhood obesity is a good thing. In one small way, Bloomberg was trying to alter the environment that tempts people to overconsume sugary drinks. His rationale was unassailable: if consumers—for example, moviegoers—aren't offered a thirty-two-ounce soft drink for a few pennies more than the sixteen-ounce cup, they'll buy the smaller version and consume less sugar. He wasn't stopping people from drinking all the sugary beverage they wanted (they could still buy *two* sixteen-ounce cups). He was merely putting up a small obstacle to alter people's behavior—like closing your door so people must knock before interrupting you.

Personally, I didn't have a dog in this race. (I am not here to judge. My mission is to help people become the person that they want to be, not tell them who that person is.) I watched Bloomberg's plan unfold purely as an exercise in the richness of our resistance to change. I love New York. The good citizens didn't disappoint.

People quickly lodged the "nanny state" objection: where does this Bloomberg fellow come off telling me how to live my life? Local politicians objected because they hadn't been consulted. They hated the mayor's high-handed methods. The NAACP objected to the mayor's hypocrisy in targeting soft drinks while cutting phys ed budgets in schools. So-called "mom-and-pop" store owners objected because the ban exempted convenience stores such as 7-Eleven, which could put the mom-and-pops out of business. Jon Stewart mocked the mayor because the two-hundred-dollar ticket for illegally selling supersize soft drinks was double the fine for selling marijuana.

And so on. In the end, after a barrage of lawsuits, a judge struck down the law for being "arbitrary and capricious." My point: even when the individual and societal benefits of changing a specific behavior are indisputable, we are geniuses at inventing reasons to avoid change. It is much easier, and more fun, to attack the strategy of the person who's trying to help than to try to solve the problem.

That genius for resisting change becomes more acute when it applies to us—when it's our turn to change how we behave. We fall back on a set of beliefs that trigger denial, resistance, and ultimately self-delusion. They are more pernicious than excuses. An excuse is the handy explanation we offer when we disappoint other people. Not merely convenient, it is often made up on the spot. We don't exercise because "it's boring" or we're "too busy." We're late for work because of "traffic" or "an emergency with the kids." We hurt someone because we "didn't have a choice." These excuses, basically variations on "The dog ate my homework," are so abused it's a wonder anyone believes us (even when we're telling the truth).

But what should we call the rationalizations we privately harbor when we disappoint ourselves? Mere "excuse" is somehow inadequate to describe these inner beliefs that represent how we interpret our world. An excuse explains why we fell short of expectations after the fact. Our inner beliefs trigger failure before it happens. They sabotage lasting change by canceling its possibility. We employ these beliefs as articles of faith to justify our inaction and then wish away the result. I call them belief triggers.

1. If I understand, I will do.

Everything that I am going to suggest in this book works. It doesn't "kind of" work or "sort of" work. It works. My suggestions will help you understand how to close the gap between the "ideal you" and the "real you." However, this does not mean that you will do it.

People who read my writing sometimes tell me, "It's common sense. I didn't read anything here that I don't already know." It's the default critique of most advice books (you may be thinking it right now). My thought is always: "True, but I'll bet that you read plenty here that you don't already do." If you've ever been to a seminar or corporate retreat where all attendees agreed on what to do next—and a year later nothing has changed—you know that there's a difference between *understanding* and *doing*. Just because people understand what to do doesn't ensure that they will actually do it. This belief triggers *confusion*.

It also pervades the fourteen belief triggers that follow. You may be familiar with them. You may think they don't apply to you. This is a belief worth questioning, too.

2. I have willpower and won't give in to temptation.

We deify willpower and self-control, and mock its absence. People who achieve through remarkable willpower are "strong" and "heroic." People who need help or structure are "weak." This is crazy—because few of us can accurately gauge or predict our willpower. We not only overestimate it, we chronically underestimate the power of triggers in our environment to lead us astray. Our environment is a magnificent willpower-reduction machine.

In *The Odyssey*, Homer's classic work from circa 800 BC, the hero Odysseus faces many perils and tests on his return home from the Trojan War. At one point his ship must pass the Sirens whose haunting voices lure sailors to their death on the rocks near shore. Odysseus wants to hear the Sirens so he puts wax in his men's ears and ties himself to the ship's mast so he can safely hear the Sirens' singing without going mad. He knew willpower alone wasn't enough to overcome the Sirens' temptation.

Unlike Odysseus, few of us foresee the challenges we will face. As a result, the willpower we assume when we set a goal rarely measures up to the willpower we display in achieving that goal. Something always comes up to sink our boat. This belief triggers *overconfidence*.

3. Today is a special day.

When we want to make an excuse for errant behavior, any day can be designated as a "special day." We yield to impulse and short-term gratification because today is the Super Bowl, or my birthday, or our anniversary, or my day off, or National Cookie Day (December 4 if you don't already know). Tomorrow is back to normal. We'll be our usual disciplined self then.

If we really want to change we have to make peace with the fact that we cannot self-exempt every time the calendar offers us a more attractive alternative to our usual day. Excusing our momentary lapses as an outlier event triggers a self-indulgent *inconsistency*—which is fatal for change. Successful change doesn't happen overnight. We're playing a long game, not the short game of instant gratification that our special day provides.

4. "At least I'm better than . . ."

In a down moment after failure or loss, we tell ourselves, "At least I'm better than _____." We award ourselves a free pass because we're not the worst in the world. This is our excuse to take it easy, lowering the bar on our motivation and discipline. Other people have to change more than we do. We've triggered a false sense of *immunity*.

5. I shouldn't need help and structure.

One of our most dysfunctional beliefs is our contempt for simplicity and structure. We believe that we are above needing structure to help us on seemingly simple tasks. For example, as Dr. Atul Gawande reported in *The Checklist Manifesto*, central line infections in intensive care units virtually disappear when doctors follow a simple five-point checklist involving rote procedures such as washing hands, cleaning the patient's skin, and using a sterile dressing after inserting the line. For many years, despite the checklist's proven success rate, doctors resisted it. After years of medical training, many doctors thought that the constant reminders, especially when delivered by subordinate nurses, were demeaning. The surgeons thought, "I shouldn't need to use a checklist to remember simple instructions."

This is a natural response that combines three competing impulses: 1) our contempt for simplicity (only complexity is worthy of our attention); 2) our contempt for instruction and follow-up; and 3) our faith, however unfounded, that we can succeed all by ourselves. In combination these three trigger an unappealing *exceptionalism* in us. When we presume that we are better than people who need structure and guidance, we lack one of the most crucial ingredients for change: humility.

6. I won't get tired and my enthusiasm will not fade.

In the morning, when we plan to work long hours and finish our assignment we are not exhausted. We may feel fresh and full of energy. But after we work several hours we become tired and more vulnerable to throwing in the towel. When we plan to achieve our goals, we believe that our energy will not flag and that we will never lose our enthusiasm for the process of change. We seldom recognize that self-control is a limited resource. As we become tired our self-control begins to waver and may eventually disappear. The sheer effort of sticking with the plan triggers *depletion*.

7. I have all the time in the world.

Here are two opposing beliefs that we simultaneously hold in our minds and mash into one warped view of time: 1) we chronically underestimate the time it takes to get anything done; 2) we believe that time is open-ended and sufficiently spacious for us to get to all our self-improvement goals eventually. (Hah! I've been promising myself that this is the year I'll read *War and Peace*—and have been promising for forty-three consecutive years.) This faith in time's infinite patience triggers *procrastination*. We will start getting better tomorrow. There's no urgency to do it today.

8. I won't get distracted and nothing unexpected will occur.

When we make plans for the future, we seldom plan on distractions. We plan as if we are going to live in a perfect world and be left alone to focus on our work. Although this state of being left alone has never happened in the past, we plan as if this nirvana-like world will surely exist in the future. We get down to work without accommodating the fact that life always intrudes to alter our priorities and test our focus.

Earning an undergraduate degree in mathematical economics taught me about the *high probability of low-probability events*. We don't plan for low-probability events because, by definition, any one of them is unlikely to occur. Who plans on a flat tire, or accident, or stalled traffic because of an overturned semi on their way to work? And yet the odds of at least one of these events occurring are high. We are all victimized, more frequently than we like, by traffic jams and flat tires and accidents. This belief triggers *unrealistic expectations*.

(Ironically, as I am typing this on a Sunday afternoon, I have just received an email from a client saying, "I have an emergency at work and need to get your considered opinion. Is there any way that we can talk now?" While the probability of *her* contacting me for an emergency talk on this particular Sunday afternoon was close to zero [she had never done this before], the probability of *some* distraction happening on Sunday afternoon is pretty high.)

In my coaching, I usually work with executive clients for eighteen months. I warn each client that the process will take longer than they expect because there will be a crisis. I can't name the crisis, but it will be legitimate and real—for example, an acquisition, a defection, a major product recall—and it may dramatically extend the time they need to achieve positive change. They cannot predict it, but they should expect it—and it will distract them and slow them down.

9. An epiphany will suddenly change my life.

An epiphany implies that change can arise out of a sudden burst of insight and willpower. It happens, of course. An alcoholic hits rock bottom. A gambler goes broke. A nasty executive is threatened with dismissal. And for a while, each of them sees the light. But more often than not, an epiphany experience triggers *magical thinking.* I'm skeptical of any "instant conversion experience." It might produce change in the short run, but nothing meaningful or lasting—because the process is based on impulse rather than strategy, hopes and prayers rather than structure.

10. My change will be permanent and I will never have to worry again.

The Great Western Disease is "I'll be happy when . . ." This is our belief that happiness is a static and finite goal, within our grasp when we get that promotion, or buy that house, or find that mate, or whatever. It's inculcated in us by the most popular story line in contemporary life: there is a person; the person spends money on a product or service; the person is eternally happy. This is called a TV commercial. The average American spends 140,000 hours watching TV commercials. Some brainwashing is inevitable. Is it any wonder that we so casually assume that any positive change we make will change us forever? It's the same with behavioral change. We set a goal and mistakenly believe that in achieving that goal we will be happy—and that we will never regress. This belief triggers a false sense of *permanence*.

If only this were true. My research involving more than 86,000 respondents around the world on changing leadership behavior, "Leadership Is a Contact Sport," paints a different picture. If we don't follow up, our positive change doesn't last. It's the difference between, say, getting in shape and staying in shape—hitting our physical conditioning goals and maintaining them. Even when we *get there*, we cannot *stay there* without commitment and discipline. We have to keep going to the gym—forever.

Fairy tales end with "and they lived happily ever after." That is why they are called fairy tales, not documentaries.

11. My elimination of old problems will not bring on new problems.

Even if we appreciate that no change will provide a permanent solution to our problems, we forget that as we usher an old problem out the door a new problem usually enters. I see this all the time with my successful clients. They all agree that the euphoria of achieving their dream job of CEO vanishes by the second meeting with the board of directors. The old problem of becoming CEO has been replaced by the new problems of being CEO. This belief triggers a fundamental misunderstanding of our *future challenges*.

Lottery winners are a notorious example here. Who hasn't imagined the worry-free bliss that comes with sudden riches? And yet, research shows that only two years after winning the lottery, the winners are not that much happier than they were before they collected their checks. The big payday solves their old problems of debt and paying the mortgage and funding their children's schooling. But new problems immediately appear. Relatives and friends and charities suddenly appear expecting a generous handout. The old problem of a cheap home in a neighborhood with old friends has been replaced with the new problem of an expensive home in a new neighborhood with no friends.

12. My efforts will be fairly rewarded.

From childhood we are brought up to believe that life is supposed to be fair. Our noble efforts and good works will be rewarded. When we are not properly rewarded we feel cheated. Our dashed expectations trigger *resentment*.

When I coach leaders, I insist that they pursue change because they believe in their hearts that it is the right thing to do. It will help them become a better leader, team member, family member—and by extension improve the lives of the people in their immediate orbit. It will help them live the values that they believe in. If they're only pursuing change for an external reward (a promotion, more money), I won't work with them because 1) there are no certainties that we'll get what we want, 2) if the reward is the only motivator people revert to their old ways, and 3) all I've done is help a phony succeed.

Getting better is its own reward. If we do that, we can never feel cheated.

13. No one is paying attention to me.

We believe that we can occasionally lapse back into bad behavior because people aren't paying close attention. We are practically invisible, triggering a dangerous preference for *isolation*. Even worse, it's only half true. While our slow and steady improvement may not be as obvious to others as it is to us, when we revert to our previous behavior, people *always* notice.

14. If I change I am "inauthentic."

Many of us have a misguided belief that how we behave today not only defines us but represents our fixed and constant selves, the authentic us forever. If we change, we are somehow not being true to who we really are. This belief triggers *stubbornness*. We refuse to adapt our behavior to new situations because "it isn't me."

For example, it is not uncommon for me to work with an executive who makes comments like, "I am no good at giving positive recognition. That's just not me." I then ask these people if they have an incurable genetic disease that is prohibiting them from giving people the recognition that they deserve.

We can change not only our behavior but how we define

ourselves. When we put ourselves in a box marked "That's not me," we ensure that we'll never get out of it.

15. I have the wisdom to assess my own behavior.

We are notoriously inaccurate in assessing ourselves. Among the more than 80,000 professionals I've asked to rate their performance, 70 percent believe they are in the top 10 percent of their peer group, 82 percent believe that they are in the top fifth, and 98.5 percent place themselves in the top half. If we're successful, we tend to credit ourselves for our victories and blame our situation or other people for our losses. This belief triggers an impaired sense of *objectivity*. It convinces us that while other people consistently overrate themselves, our own self-assessment is fair and accurate.

| | |

Overconfidence. Stubbornness. Magical thinking. Confusion. Resentment. Procrastination. That's a lot of heavy baggage to carry on our journey of change.

All these rationalizations, some profound, some silly, still don't completely answer the larger question, *Why don't we become the person we want to be?* Why do we plan to be a better person one day—and then abandon that plan within hours or days?

There is an even larger reason that explains why we don't make the changes we want to make—greater than the high quality of our excuses or our devotion to our belief triggers. It's called the environment.

Chapter 3

It's the Environment

Most of us go through life unaware of how our environment shapes our behavior.

When we experience "road rage" on a crowded freeway, it's not because we're sociopathic monsters. It's because the temporary condition of being behind the wheel in a car, surrounded by rude impatient drivers, triggers a change in our otherwise placid demeanor. We've unwittingly placed ourselves in an environment of impatience, competitiveness, and hostility—and it alters us.

When we take highly vocal umbrage at disappointing food in a restaurant by abusing a friendly waiter and making nasty comments to the maître d'—neither of whom cooked the food—it's not because we regularly display the noblesse oblige of Louis XIV. Our behavior is an aberration, triggered by a restaurant environment where we believe that paying handsomely for a meal entitles us to royal treatment. In an environment of entitlement, we behave accordingly. Outside the restaurant we resume our lives as model citizens—patient, polite, not entitled.

Even when we're aware of our environment and welcome being in it, we become victims of its ruthless power. Three decades ago, when I started spending half my days on airplanes, I regarded being on a plane as the ideal environment for reading and writing. No phones, no screens, no interruptions. The constant travel wasn't an annoyance—because it allowed me to be hyperproductive. But as the airlines' in-flight entertainment offerings gradually expanded from one film on a single screen to universal Wi-Fi and fifty on-demand channels at my seat, my productivity dropped. What had been a pocket of monastic serenity had become a glittering arcade of distraction. And I was tempted and easily distracted. Instead of getting work done or catching up on much-needed sleep while crossing several time zones, I'd watch two or three pointless movies in a row. Each time as I walked off the plane, instead of being happy to arrive safely on the ground, ready to charge into my next assignment, I berated myself over the time I'd wasted in flight. I felt that I had dropped the ball on being disciplined. I also noticed that where in the past I'd leave the airport feeling relaxed and rested, I was now more tired and enervated. It took me a couple of years to realize that the onboard environment had changed—and I had changed with it. But not for the better.

If there is one "disease" that I'm trying to cure in this book, it revolves around our total misapprehension of our environment. We think we are in sync with our environment, but actually it's at war with us. We think we control our environment but in fact it controls us. We think our external environment is conspiring in our favor—that is, helping us—

when actually it is taxing and draining us. It is not interested in what it can give us. It's only interested in what it can take from us.

If it sounds like I'm treating our environment as a hostile character in our life dramas, that's intentional. I want us to think of our environment as if it were a person—as imminent and real as an archrival sitting across the table. Our environment is not merely the amorphous space just beyond our fingertips and skin, our corporeal being. It's not a given like the air around us, something we inhale and exhale but otherwise ignore as we go about our routines. Our environment is a nonstop triggering mechanism whose impact on our behavior is too significant to be ignored. Regarding it as a flesh-and-blood character is not just fanciful metaphor. It's a strategy that lets us finally see what we're up against. (In some cases, I advise giving our environment a name.)

It's not all bad. Our environment can be the angel on our shoulder, making us a better person—like when we find ourselves at a wedding or class reunion or awards dinner and the joyous spark of fellow feeling in the room overwhelms people. Everyone is hugging and promising to stay in touch and get together real soon. (Of course, that feeling often fades the moment we return to our regular lives—in other words, find ourselves in a different environment. We are altered by the change. We forget our promises. We don't follow up. We don't stay in touch. The contrast couldn't be more stark. One environment elevates us, the other erases the good vibes as if they never happened.)

Much of the time, however, our environment is the devil. That's the part that eludes us: entering a new environment changes our behavior in sly ways, whether we're sitting in a conference room with colleagues or visiting friends for dinner or enduring our weekly phone call with an aging parent.

For example, my wife, Lyda, and I are not cynical people. Although it's my job to point out people's personal challenges during the workweek, in my "civilian" life I try to be a non-judgmental guy. I make a conscious effort to accept people's foibles and "let it go." Lyda doesn't have to work as hard as I do at tolerance; she's always the kindest person in the room. Yet we become different people whenever we have dinner with our neighbors Terry and John. They are a droll, amusing couple, but their humor stems from a sour worldview. Nearly everything that comes out of their mouths—about mutual friends or political figures or the neighbors' pets—is cynical and snarky, almost cruel, as if they were auditioning for a celebrity roast. As Lyda and I debriefed after one particularly mean-spirited dinner, we marveled at the sarcastic comments *we* made. It wasn't like us. We searched for reasons for our unusual behavior, concluding that the only variable was the people we were with and the setting we found ourselves in. In other words, the environment. In the same way that people talk more softly with a soft-spoken person, more quickly with a fast talker, our opinions were fundamentally altered inside the dark conversational bubble created by Terry and John.

Sometimes altering one factor can turn an ideal environment into a disaster. It doesn't change us. It changes everyone else in the room and how they react to us. Many years ago I was speaking at an off-site gathering of partners from a consulting firm. Although my previous work with this firm had gone well, this time something wasn't working. No give-and-take, no lively laughter, just a group of very smart people sitting on their hands. I finally realized that the room was too hot. Amazingly, by merely turning down the temperature in the room, the session got back on track. Like a rock star demanding red M&Ms in the dressing room, I'm now a bit of a diva about insisting on a cool environment for my presentations. I've learned how one tweak in the environment changes everything.*

The most pernicious environments are the ones that compel us to compromise our sense of right and wrong. In the ultracompetitive environment of the workplace, it can happen to the most solid citizens.

I remember working at a European conglomerate with a top-performing executive named Karl. He had a dictatorial management style—obsessive, strict, and punitive. He was openly gunning for the CEO job, and he drove his staff mercilessly to further his career. His mantra was "Make your number." He'd write off anyone who contradicted his "number" or said it was unrealistic. To those who remained loyal, he'd scream, "Do whatever it takes!" Not surprisingly, his team started taking shortcuts to make their numbers. Some went from borderline unethical to clearly unethical behavior. In the environment Karl created, they didn't see it as moral erosion. They saw it as the only option on the table.

Eventually, the truth came out. The scandal cost the company tens of millions of euros and even more in reputational

---

*I've since learned that David Letterman lowered his *Late Show* studio temperature to a chilly 55 degrees before going onstage. He experimented with room temperatures in the 1980s and discovered that his jokes worked best at 55 degrees, which makes the sound crisper and the audience more alert.

damage. Karl's defense was, "I never asked my people to do anything immoral or illegal." He didn't need to ask. The environment he created did the work for him.

Our environment changes us even when we're dealing one-on-one with people to whom we'd ordinarily show kindness. We turn friends into strangers, behaving as if we'll never have to face them again.

I was conducting a 360-degree feedback survey with a woman named Jackie about her company's chief operating officer some years ago when she and I got sidetracked into a discussion about the emotional toll of her job. Jackie sounded like she wanted to unload some deep issues, so I listened. She was an in-house lawyer at a sales organization, specializing in employment matters. One of her duties was to negotiate separation agreements with departing sales executives, whether they were leaving of their own volition or not.

"It's not my favorite part of the job," she said. "I'm dealing with people at a fragile moment in their careers. Most of them have no immediate prospects. And I represent the company's interests, not theirs."

Jackie specifically wanted to talk about an executive who'd been let go. She'd gone to college with the man, reconnected with him after they began working at the same company. They talked on a regular basis, occasionally socialized. It was Jackie's job to hash out the terms of his departure. The severance package was contractual and generous. The negotiable part was determining how much of the ongoing revenue stream from the man's sales accounts would go to him and how much to the company.

For reasons she couldn't articulate, Jackie took a hard position with the man. Over several weeks of back-and-forth emails and phone calls, she used all her negotiating wiles and leverage to ensure that the company got the lion's share of sales commissions from the man's accounts.

At first, I didn't see why she was telling me this. "You were doing your job, being a professional," I said. But she was clearly troubled by the memory of her behavior.

"That's what I tell myself," said Jackie. "But this man was my friend. He deserved some compassion. Instead, I argued with him over a grand total of twenty thousand dollars, a sum of money that wouldn't have made a dent on the company's bottom line but would be significant to a jobless friend. Who was I trying to impress? The company didn't care. It's the most painful regret of my career."

I'd like to report that I had wise and consoling words for her that day. But this happened about ten years ago and the environment's malign power wasn't obvious to me at the time.

I see it now, of course. As a lawyer, Jackie was trained to be adversarial. She was accustomed to arguing and negotiating over minor deal points. In a sales environment where everyone's measuring who's up, who's down, who's squeezing the last dime out of a deal, Jackie wanted to show she was doing her part. It demonstrated her value to the company. Unfortunately, that same ruthless bottom-line environment fostered the aggressive behavior that blurred right and wrong for Jackie. In her zeal to be a professional negotiator, she behaved like an amateur human being.

Some environments are designed precisely to lure us into acting against our interest. That's what happens when we overspend at the high-end mall. Blame it on a retail experience specifically engineered—from the lighting to the color schemes to the width of the aisles—to maximize our desire and liberate cash from our wallets. What's really strange is that the mall environment doesn't jump out at us like a thief in a dark alley. We have *chosen* to place ourselves in an environment that, based on past experience, will trigger the urge to buy something we neither need nor want. (This is even more predictable if we go without a specific shopping list—and put ourselves at the mercy of random, undisciplined consumption and a vague feeling that we can't leave the mall empty-handed.) In overspending we fall into a trap that we have set for ourselves. The environments of a casino or an online shopping site are even less safe. Very smart people have spent their waking hours with one goal in mind: designing each detail so it triggers a customer to stay and spend.

Other environments are not as manipulative and predatory as a luxury store. But they're still not working *for* us. Consider the perennial goal of getting a good night's sleep. Insufficient sleep is practically a national epidemic, afflicting one-third of American adults (it's twice as bad for teenagers).

Sleep should be easy to achieve.

We have the *motivation* to sleep well. Who doesn't want to wake up alert rather than foggy, refreshed rather than sluggish?

We *understand* how much sleep we need. It's basic arithmetic. If we have work or class early the next morning and need six to eight hours of sleep, we should work backward and plan on going to bed around 11 p.m.

And we have *control*: Sleep is a self-regulated activity that happens in an environment totally governed by us—our home. We decide when to tuck in for the night. We choose our environment, from the room, to the bed, to the sheets and pillows.

So why don't we do what we know is good for us? Why do we stay up later than is good for us—and in turn not get enough sleep and wake up tired rather than refreshed?

I blame it on a fundamental misunderstanding of how our environment shapes our behavior. It leads to a phenomenon that Dutch sleep researchers at Utrecht University call "bedtime procrastination." We put off going to bed at the intended time because we prefer to remain in our current environment—watching a late-night movie or playing video games or cleaning the kitchen—rather than move to the relative calm and comfort of our bedroom. It's a choice between competing environments.

But because we don't appreciate how our environment influences our choice, we fail to make the right choice (that is, go to bed). We continue doing what we're doing, victims of inertia, unaware that getting a good night's sleep is not something we deserve because we're tired but rather something we must earn by developing better habits. If we understood how our environment can sabotage our sleep habits, we'd change our behavior. We'd stop what we're doing, turn off our cell phones and iPads and laptops, banish the TV from the bedroom, and turn in for the night—as if we planned it.

How we learn to change our behavior from bad habits to good ones, through discipline rather than occasional good fortune, is the subject matter—and promise—of this book's remaining pages.

But first, I have one more piece of disturbing news. Our environment isn't static. It alters throughout our day. It's a moving target, easy to miss.

If we think about our environment at all, we probably regard it as an expansive macrosphere that is defined by the major influences on our behavior—our family, our job, our schooling, our friends and colleagues, the neighborhood we live in, the physical space we work in. It's like a borderless nation-state bearing our name that reminds us who we are but has no influence on our decisions or actions.

If only that were true.

The environment that I'm most concerned with is actually smaller, more particular than that. It's *situational*, and it's a hyperactive shape-shifter. Every time we enter a new situation, with its mutating who-what-when-where-and-why specifics, we are surrendering ourselves to a new environment—and putting our goals, our plans, our behavioral integrity at risk. It's a simple dynamic: a changing environment changes us.

The mother who, in the environment of her home, lei-surely makes breakfast for herself and her kids before sending them off to school and transporting herself to work is not the same person who, immediately upon arriving at the office, walks into a major budget meeting headed by her company's founder. There's no way she could be. At home she is more or less chief of her domain—and exhibits the behavior of an ultra-responsible leader, caring for her family, expecting obedience, assuming respect. It's a different environment at the office. She may still be the same confident and competent person she was at home. But, wittingly or not, she fine-tunes her behavior in the meeting. She's deferential to authority. She pays close attention to the statements and body language of her colleagues. And so it goes through her workday, from sit-uation to situation. As the environment changes, so does she.

There's nothing inauthentic about the woman's behavior. It's a necessary survival strategy in a professional environment, especially if you're no longer in total command of your situation.

It wouldn't be any different if this same woman were the head of the company. Leaders alter their behavior to suit the environment, too. The head of a major construction firm once told me that as an active defense contractor, with differing levels of security clearances for different government contracts, she had to be incredibly scrupulous about the information she shared across parts of her company. She was required by the federal government to compartmentalize what she said. She could share sensitive information over here but not over there, and vice versa. As a result, she was hyperalert to the link between her environment and behavior (failure to do so could not only hurt her company but land her in prison).

As an exercise, I asked her to track her environment and how many behavioral personas she adopted as she went through a typical day. Nine, she reported back. She behaved like a CEO among her office staff, a public speaker at a PR event, an engineer among her design wizards, a saleswoman with a potential customer, a diplomat with a visiting trade group, and so on. Few of us are legally mandated to be so aware.

This situational aspect of our environment is what I've been working on with my one-on-one coaching clients. It's not that these very smart executives don't know that circumstances change from moment to moment as they go through their day. They know. But at the level these people operate in—where nine out of ten times they are the most powerful person in the room—they can easily start believing they're immune to the environment's ill will. In a frenzy of delusion, they actually believe they control their environment, not the other way around. Given all the deference and fawning these C-level executives experience throughout the day, such misguided belief is understandable. Not acceptable, but understandable.

For example, in 2008 I was hired to coach an executive named Nadeem in London. A Pakistani by birth, Nadeem had emigrated to the United Kingdom as a child, graduated from the London School of Economics, and had risen to one of the top five positions at a leading consumer goods company. Nadeem had all the virtues of a rising star being groomed for CEO. He was smart, personable, hardworking, respected (even "loved") by his direct reports. But some chinks in his nice-guy reputation had appeared. I was asked by the CEO to smooth them out.

We all know people who get on our nerves and induce us to behave badly. Around such people, we're edgy, nasty, combative, rude, and constantly apologizing for our uncharacteristic behavior—though we rarely attribute the cause of our errant behavior to such people. It was the same for Nadeem. When I interviewed his colleagues, a recurring theme came up. Nadeem was a great guy, but he lost his cool whenever he was in a public forum with Simon the chief marketing officer.

I asked Nadeem what his issues were with Simon. "He is a racist," he said.

"Is that your opinion, or can you back it up with proof?" I asked.

"My opinion," he said. "But if I feel it, isn't it a fact, too?"

My feedback had said that Simon loved to bait Nadeem in meetings. It wasn't racial. Simon was a self-entitled "toff," a product of Britain's privileged class and elite schools. He had a penchant for pomposity and biting remarks. The sarcasm was his way of reminding people of his background, elevating himself while diminishing others. He wasn't a fun guy to be with, but he was not a bigot.

Nadeem overreacted to Simon. When Simon challenged him in a meeting, Nadeem felt that, given the decades of racial resentment and tension between Brits and Pakistanis, he couldn't be seen as backing down.

"If I take his crap, it makes me look weak," said Nadeem. So he fought back.

In Nadeem's mind it was a racial issue, but he was the only one who interpreted it that way. Nadeem's colleagues saw him as a vocal proponent of teamwork who wasn't modeling what he was preaching. It was branding Nadeem as a phony.

My task was to make Nadeem see that

- his behavior wasn't serving him well;
- it was isolated to the time he spent in Simon's presence;
- it was triggered whenever Simon challenged him, and
- he had to change because he couldn't count on Simon to change.

The big insight for Nadeem was that his behavior was situational, triggered solely by Simon. Every time Nadeem found himself in the "Simon environment" (that's what he named it), he would go on high alert. It was a new level of mindfulness for him—and a critical (though not the only) factor in his swift change for the better.

We'll come back to Nadeem in Chapter 20 to learn precisely how he changed his behavior and, in turn, won back the respect of his colleagues and his nemesis, Simon. It's an uplifting story with a shocking admission from Nadeem—and (spoiler alert) it neatly encapsulates the most important benefit of adult behavioral change.

But for now let's absorb and wallow in Nadeem's hard-won appreciation that our environment is a relentless triggering machine. If we do not create and control our environment, our environment creates and controls us. And the result turns us into someone we do not recognize.

Chapter 4

Identifying Our Triggers

As Nadeem's coach, I had the luxury of interviewing his colleagues and direct reports and hearing the unvarnished truth about his behavior. I was accumulating valuable feedback that Nadeem wasn't in a position to get.

A little prodding is required at the start of each interview, because people are essentially decent and kind. They don't want to hurt a colleague's feelings, or appear catty. Sometimes they're afraid of retribution, despite the cloak of anonymity I provide. But eventually people realize that this process is in everyone's best interest, so they tell the truth.

The interviewees almost always focus on my client's good or bad behavior that they have experienced personally. Interviewees rarely mention the environment in which that behavior occurs. I have to press for that information. *When does he act like this? With whom? Why?* Eventually I get useful answers. The interviewees begin describing my client behaving badly in situational terms such as when he's "under pressure" or "racing a deadline" or "juggling too many balls." Slowly it

dawns on them how profoundly the environment affects behavior.*

That's what happened with Nadeem's feedback. His colleagues described Nadeem's defensiveness in meetings. But it
took insistent questioning before they associated it exclusively
with Simon's presence in the room.

Feedback—both the act of giving it and taking it—is
our first step in becoming smarter, more mindful about
the connection between our environment and our behavior.
Feedback teaches us to see our environment as a triggering mechanism. In some cases, the feedback itself is the
trigger.

Consider, for example, all the feedback we get when we're
behind the wheel of a car, how we ignore some of it, and why
only some of it actually triggers desirable behavior.

Say you're driving down a country road at the posted speed
limit of 55 mph, approaching a village. You know this because
a half mile outside the village a sign says, SPEED ZONE AHEAD
30 MPH. The sign is just a warning, not a command to slow
down, so you maintain your speed. Thirty seconds later, you
reach the village, where the sign says, SPEED LIMIT 30 MPH.
You may comply, but if you're like most drivers you'll maintain your speed (or slow down slightly) because you've been
driving on autopilot in a 55-mph environment and it's easier to continue doing what you're doing than to stop doing it.
Only if you see a manned police car monitoring motorists'

---

*Of course, the interviewees rarely make the logical leap and apply
the insight to themselves. At least not after one interview that is *not*
about them.

speeds will you comply with the mandated 30 mph—because a police officer handing out speeding tickets represents an unwanted consequence to you.

Every community in the developed world has to deal with speeding drivers putting citizens at risk. For years drivers in my neighborhood north of San Diego ignored the speed signs that told them to slow down as they transitioned from the 65 mph on the San Diego Freeway to 45 mph on the main commercial thoroughfares and 30 mph in school zones and residential neighborhoods. Nothing worked to decrease speeding, not even a greater police ticketing presence, until town officials installed radar speed displays (RSDs)—a speed limit sign posted above a digital readout measuring "Your Speed." You've probably seen them on your town's streets near a school or as you approach a tollbooth. If the RSD says you're speeding, you've probably stepped on the brake immediately. As sensor technology becomes cheaper, RSDs are being more widely used so the data about their effectiveness is deeper and more reliable. Speed limit compliance increases 30 to 60 percent with RSDs—and the effect lasts with drivers for several miles beyond the RSD.

Radar speed displays—also called driver feedback systems—work because they harness a well-established concept in behavior theory called a feedback loop. The RSDs measure a driver's action (that is, speeding) and relay the information to the driver in real time, inducing the driver to react. It's a loop of action, information, reaction. When the reaction is measured, a new loop begins, and so on and so on. Given the immediate change in a driver's behavior after just one glance at an RSD, it's easy to imagine the immense utility of feedback loops in changing people's behavior.

A feedback loop comprises four stages: evidence, relevance, consequence, and action. Once you recognize this, it's easy to see why the radar speed displays' exploitation of the loop works so well. Drivers get data about their speed in real time (evidence). The information gets their attention because it's coupled with the posted speed limit, indicating whether they're obeying or breaking the law (relevance). Aware that they're speeding, drivers fear getting a ticket or hurting someone (consequence). So they slow down (action).

I'm basically initiating a feedback loop at the start of any one-on-one coaching assignment. My first stage with Nadeem, for example, was presenting him with the *evidence*—the interviews that I had compiled and shared with him. The stories about his behavior were emotionally resonant for Nadeem because they were coming from people he respected. They had unequivocal *relevance*. The loop's third stage, *consequence*, was patently obvious: if Nadeem didn't change his behavior around Simon, he was not behaving as the team member he wanted to be, and potentially damaging his career. It wasn't a difficult choice. Once the evidence, relevance, and consequence were firmly lodged in Nadeem's mind, he had sufficient clarity to close the loop with *action*. He would ignore Simon's provocateuring ways. He would resist sparring with Simon. He would win Simon over and, in turn, reclaim his colleague's respect and his own reputation. Each time he displayed restraint with Simon, he got a little better, a little more confident that he was on the right track and making a better impression on his colleagues. And the loop could run again, a prior action leading to a new action nudging Nadeem ever closer to his goal.

This is how feedback ultimately triggers desirable behavior. Once we deconstruct feedback into its four stages of evidence, relevance, consequence, and action, the world never looks the same again. Suddenly we understand that our good behavior is not random. It's logical. It follows a pattern. It makes sense. It's within our control. It's something we can repeat. It's why some obese people finally—and instantly—take charge of their eating habits when they're told that they have diabetes and will die or go blind or lose a limb if they don't make a serious lifestyle change. Death, blindness, and loss of limb are consequences we understand and can't brush aside.

I don't want to get lost in theory over feedback loops. They're complex and can be applied to almost anything. Photosynthesis is a feedback loop between the sun and plants. Owners of hybrid cars (like me in my Ford C-Max) are in a feedback loop when they obsessively check their dashboard's gas consumption display and adjust their driving to maximize gas mileage (they're called "hypermilers"). The Cold War arms race, with East and West escalating weaponry to match each other, may be the most expensive feedback loop in history.

For our purposes, let's focus on the feedback loop created by our environment and our behavior.

As a trigger, our environment has the *potential* to resemble a feedback loop. After all, our environment is constantly providing new information that has meaning and consequence for us and alters our behavior. But the resemblance ends there. Where a well-designed feedback loop triggers desirable behavior, our environment often triggers bad behavior, and it does so against our will and better judgment and without our awareness. We don't know we've changed.

Which brings up the obvious question (well, obvious to me): *What if we could control our environment so it triggered our most desired behavior—like an elegantly designed feedback loop?* Instead of blocking us from our goals, this environment propels us. Instead of dulling us to our surroundings, it sharpens us. Instead of shutting down who we are, it opens us.

To achieve that, we first have to clarify the term *trigger*:

A behavioral trigger is any stimulus that impacts our behavior.

Within that broad definition there are several distinctions that improve our understanding of how triggers influence our behavior.

1. A behavioral trigger can be direct or indirect.

Direct triggers are stimuli that immediately and obviously impact behavior, with no intermediate steps between the triggering event and your response. You see a happy baby and smile. A child chases a basketball into the street in front of your car and you instantly hit the brakes. *Indirect triggers* take a more circuitous route before influencing behavior. You see a family photo that initiates a series of thoughts that compel you to pick up the phone and call your sister.

2. A trigger can be internal or external.

External triggers come from the environment, bombarding our five senses as well as our minds. *Internal triggers* come from thoughts or feelings that are not connected with any outside stimulus. Many people meditate to dampen the internal trigger they refer to as an "inner voice." Likewise, the idea that inexplicably pops into your head when you're alone musing on a problem is an internal trigger inspiring you to take action. Its origin may be a mystery, but if it stimulates behavior, it's as valid as any external prompt.

3. A trigger can be conscious or unconscious.

Conscious triggers require awareness. You know why your finger recoils when you touch the hot plate. *Unconscious triggers* shape your behavior beyond your awareness. For example, no matter how much people talk about the weather they're usually oblivious about its triggering influence on their moods. Respondents to the question "How happy are you?" claimed to be happier on a perfect weather day than respondents to the same question on a nasty weather day. Yet when asked, most respondents denied the weather had any impact on their scores. The weather was an unconscious trigger that changed their scores but was outside their awareness.

4. A trigger can be anticipated or unexpected.

We see *anticipated triggers* coming a mile away. For example, at the beginning of the Super Bowl, we hear the national anthem and expect raucous cheering as it ends. The song triggers a predictable response. (It works the other way, too. We know that our demeaning language will trigger other people's anger so we avoid it.) *Unanticipated triggers* take us by surprise, and as a result stimulate unfamiliar behavior. My friend Phil did not see his fall down the stairs coming, but the fall triggered a powerful desire to change.

5. A trigger can be encouraging or discouraging.

Encouraging triggers push us to maintain or expand what we are doing. They are reinforcing. The sight of a finish line for an exhausted marathon runner encourages him to keep running, even speed up. So does the appearance of a rival runner at his side about to pass him. *Discouraging triggers* push us to stop or reduce what we are doing. If we're talking in a theater, an annoyed "Ssshhh" from an audience member triggers an awareness that we're disturbing people—and we stop talking.

6. A trigger can be productive or counterproductive.

This is the most important distinction. Productive triggers push us toward becoming the person we want to be. Counterproductive triggers pull us away.

Triggers are not inherently "good" or "bad." What matters is our response to them. For example, well-meaning and supportive parents can trigger a positive self-image for one child yet be viewed as "smothering" by another child. Parents of two or more children know this all too well. Equal levels of devotion and caring can trigger gratitude in one child and rebellion in another. Same parents. Same triggers. Different responses.

To fully appreciate the reason for this, it's helpful to take a closer look at these last two dimensions of triggers— encouraging or discouraging, productive or counterproductive. They express the timeless tension between *what we want* and *what we need*. We want short-term gratification while we need long-term benefit. And we never get a break from choosing one or the other. It's the defining conflict of adult behavioral change. And we write the definitions.

We define what makes a trigger encouraging. One man's treat is another man's poison. The sudden appearance of a bowl of Rocky Road ice cream may trigger hunger in us and disgust in our lactose-intolerant dinner companion.

Likewise, we define what makes a trigger productive. We all claim to want financial security; it's a universal goal. But when we get our year-end bonus, some of us bank the money while others gamble it away over a weekend. Same trigger, same goal, different response.

We can illustrate this conflict in the following matrix where encouraging triggers lead us toward what we want and productive triggers lead us toward what we need. If only our encouraging triggers and productive triggers were the same. It can happen. It's the ideal situation. Unfortunately, what we want often lures us away from what we need. Let's take a closer look.

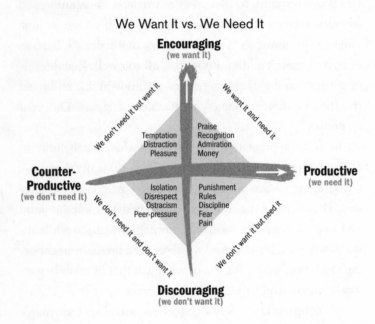

We Want It vs. We Need It

Encouraging
(we want it)

We don't need it but want it

We want it and need it

Temptation
Distraction
Pleasure

Praise
Recognition
Admiration
Money

Counter-Productive
(we don't need it)

Productive
(we need it)

We don't need it and don't want it

Isolation
Disrespect
Ostracism
Peer-pressure

Punishment
Rules
Discipline
Fear
Pain

We don't want it but need it

Discouraging
(we don't want it)

We Want It and Need It: The upper right quadrant is where we'd prefer to be all the time. It is the realm where encouraging triggers intersect with productive triggers, where the short-term gratification we want is congruent with the long-term achievement we need. Praise, recognition, admiration, and monetary rewards are common triggers here. They make us try harder right now and they also reinforce continuing behavior that drives us toward our goals. We want them now and need them later.

We Don't Need It but Want It: The paradoxical effect of an encouraging trigger that is counterproductive comes to a head most tellingly in the upper left quadrant. This is where we encounter pleasurable situations that can tempt or distract us from achieving our goals. If you've ever binge-watched a season or two of a TV show on Netflix when you should be studying, or finishing an assignment, or going to sleep, you know how an appealing distraction can trigger a self-defeating choice. You've sacrificed your goals for short-term gratification. If you've ever taken a supervisor's compliment or a client's reassurances as an excuse to ease up a little bit, you know how positive reinforcement can set you back rather than propel you ahead.

We Don't Want It but Need It: The lower right quadrant is a thorny grab bag of discouraging triggers that we don't want but that we know we need.

Rules (or any highly structured environment) are discouraging because they limit us; they exist to erase specific behaviors from our repertoire. But we need them because obeying rules makes us do the right thing. Rules push us in the right direction even when our first impulse is to go the other way.

Fear—of shame, punishment, reprisal, regret, disrespect, ostracism—is a hugely discouraging trigger, often appearing after we fail to follow a rule. If you've ever been dressed down in public by a high-ranking manager, you know it's something you don't want to repeat—which makes it a powerful motivator to stay true to your long-term goals.

Even quirky discipline can be found here. When I fine my clients twenty dollars for cynicism and sarcasm, I'm introducing a discouraging trigger (it's loss aversion, the concept that we hate losing one dollar more than we enjoy gaining two) that also aims to trigger productive behavior (that is, make people nicer).

Pain, of course, is the ultimate discouraging trigger: we immediately stop a behavior that hurts.

We Don't Need It and Don't Want It: The lower left quadrant, where our triggers are both discouraging and counterproductive, is not a good place to be. It includes all the dead-end situations that make us miserable—and we can't see any way out of them. It could be a toxic workplace or a violent neighborhood, the kinds of environment that trigger unhealthy behavior steering us away from our goals. There's not much mystery to why these ugly environments trigger fatigue, stress, apathy, hopelessness, isolation, and anger. The only puzzle is why we choose to stay here instead of fleeing at high speed.

I'm not rigid or doctrinaire about these quadrants. Our experience is too rich and fluid to be contained in a theoretical box. Some triggers overlap or mutate, depending on how we respond, and move us from a bad place to a good one. Consider the triggering impact of peer pressure. An academically ambitious teen may be mocked and ostracized by his slacker classmates for studying hard and wanting to go to college. If he allows the peer pressure to discourage him from his goals, he'll find himself in the unenviable lower left quadrant. On the other hand, if he resists the peer pressure and endures the ostracism, the isolation may focus him and steel his resolve. It gives him the discipline he needs. It may not be pleasant in the short term but it's all the push he needs to shift to the lower right quadrant. Same trigger and goals, different responses and outcomes.

I find the grid useful as an analytical tool with my clients. It enables them to take inventory of the triggers in their lives, which, if nothing else, increases their awareness about their environment. More important, it reveals whether they're operating in a productive quadrant. The right side of the matrix is where successful people want to be, moving forward on their behavioral goals.

Now it's your turn. Try this modest exercise.

Pick a behavioral goal you're still pursuing. We all have a few, from getting in shape to being a more patient parent to being more assertive around pushy people.

List the people and situations that influence the quality of your performance. Don't list all the triggers in your day; that's overkill given the hundreds, perhaps thousands of sensory and cerebral stimuli we encounter. Stick to the trigger or two that relate to one specific goal. Then define them. Are they encouraging or discouraging, productive or counterproductive?

Then chart the triggers to see if you're on the right side. If you're falling short of your goal, this simple exercise will tell you why. You're getting too much of what you want, not enough of what you need.

You might learn that your best friend at work, the kind who drops by your desk several times a day and wants to join up regularly after work, is the trigger that distracts you from going home in time to see your kids. (You need to "fire" that friend for a while.)

You might learn that you regularly miss your early morning workout because you waste your wake-up hours on Facebook or checking emails. You need the former, want the latter obviously. (You need to rethink whether morning is your optimal time to work out.)

My hope for this exercise is that it 1) makes us smarter about specific triggers and 2) helps us connect them directly to our behavioral successes and failures.

I do it myself. For example, like half the men I know, I'd be happier if I were ten pounds lighter. I've believed this for thirty years. Yet in all that time I've done nothing about those last ten pounds. Why have I failed to become the person I want to be?

The grid provides an answer.

I'm not exposed to any encouraging triggers pushing me toward the goal. I only worry out loud about the weight with my wife, Lyda. But when I do so, she showers me with positive reinforcement. "You look fine," she says. Encouraging words, but not the kind driving me in the right direction. She's not lying to make me feel better. I'm not overweight, never have been. My suit size and waistline haven't changed in decades. She's reassuring me that my weight is "good enough." So I tell myself, "She's right. Why am I beating myself over ten pounds no one notices?" As a result, I do nothing. I settle for the status quo.

I also don't have any discouraging triggers pushing me toward the goal. No one's shaming me or threatening to punish me about those last ten pounds. I haven't set up any systems of rules or fines to nudge me toward this goal. I simply don't exist on the right side of the matrix. And the right side is the only place to be for achieving behavioral change.

As insights go, locating myself on the wrong side of the matrix is a small and humbling lesson, reminding me that a trigger is a problem only if my response to it creates a problem.

To lose the ten pounds, it's up to me to escape the upper left quadrant where I prefer what I want to what I need. It's my choice, my responsibility. It doesn't solve the puzzle of achieving behavioral change, but it's a start in the right direction.

This may be the greatest payoff of identifying and defining our triggers—as the occasional but necessary reminder that, no matter how extreme the circumstances, when it comes to our behavior, we always have a choice.

Chapter 5

How Triggers Work

We always have a choice. That's not so clear-cut when the subject is triggers and our response to them. The terms *trigger* and *response* suggest an uninterrupted A-to-B sequence with no breathing room for hesitation, reflection, and choice. Is that true? Are we so easily triggered? How does a trigger actually work within us? Are there moving parts between the trigger and the behavior. If so, what are they?

When I was getting my doctorate at UCLA, the classic sequencing template for analyzing problem behavior in children was known as ABC, for antecedent, behavior, and consequence.

The antecedent is the event that prompts the behavior. The behavior creates a consequence. A common classroom example: a student is drawing pictures instead of working on the class assignment. The teacher asks the child to finish the task (the request is the antecedent). The child reacts by throwing a tantrum (behavior). The teacher responds by sending the student to the principal's office (consequence). That's the ABC sequence: *teacher request* to *child's tantrum* to *hello principal*. Armed with this insight, after several repeat episodes the teacher concludes that the child's behavior is a ploy to avoid class assignments.

In his engaging book, *The Power of Habit*, Charles Duhigg applied this ABC template to breaking and forming habits. Instead of *antecedent, behavior,* and *consequence,* he used the terms *cue, routine,* and *reward* to describe the three-part sequence known as a habit loop. Smoking cigarettes is a habit loop consisting of stress (cue), nicotine stimulation (routine), leading to temporary psychic well-being (reward). People often gain weight when they try to quit smoking because they substitute food for nicotine as their routine. In doing so, they are obeying Duhigg's Golden Rule of Habit Change—keep the cue and reward, change the routine—but they are doing it poorly. Doing thirty push-ups (or anything physically challenging) might be more effective than eating more.

Duhigg provides a terse, vivid example of the cue-routine-reward loop in action—and how we can use it to break a bad habit. A graduate student named Mandy bites her nails, habitually and incessantly until they bleed. She wants to stop. A therapist elicits from Mandy that she brings her fingers to her mouth whenever she feels a little bit of tension in her fingers. The tension appears when she's bored. That's the cue:

tension in her fingers brought on by boredom. Biting her nails is the routine that fights her boredom. The physical stimulation, especially the sense of completeness when she nibbles all ten nails down to the quick, is Mandy's reward. She craves it, which makes it habitual.

The therapist instructs Mandy to carry an index card and make a check mark on the card each time she feels the finger tension. A week later she returns to the therapist with twenty-eight check marks on the card, but she is now enlightened about the cues that send her fingers to her mouth. She's ready to replace her routine. The therapist teaches her a "competing response"—in this case, putting her hands in her pockets or gripping a pencil, anything that prevents her fingers from going to her mouth. Eventually Mandy learns to rub her arms or rap her knuckles on a desk as a substitute for the physical gratification that nail biting provides. The cue and reward stay the same. The routine has changed. A month later, Mandy has stopped biting her nails completely. She's replaced a harmful habit with a harmless one.

I don't take issue with the first and third segments of Duhigg's habit loop, whatever terms we use—*antecedent and consequence, cue and reward, stimulus and response, cause and effect, trigger and outcome*. I want to modify the middle part—the routine. The habit loop makes it sound as if all we need is an awareness of our cues so we can automatically respond with an appropriate behavior.

That's fine with habits. But when we're changing interpersonal behavior, we're adding a layer of complexity in the form of *other people*. Our triggered response can't always be automatic and unthinking and habitual—because as caring human beings we have to consider how people will respond to our actions. The fingernail doesn't care if we bite it or leave it alone. The glass of wine doesn't care if we drink it or spurn it. The cigarette is indifferent to our craving for it. But the people in our lives care enormously whether we yield to our first unwelcome impulse (for example, rudeness, cruelty, rage) or we stifle the impulse and come up with a better choice. With people in the mix, mere habit can't guide our behavior. We must be adaptable, not habitual—because the stakes are so much higher. If I surrender to my nicotine craving and smoke a cigarette, I hurt myself. If I lose my temper with my child, I hurt my child.

In the matter of adult behavioral change, I'd like to propose a modification to the sequence of antecedent, behavior, and consequence—by interrupting it with a sense of awareness and an infinitesimal stoppage of time. My modified sequence looks like this:

I've isolated three eye-blink moments—first the impulse, then the awareness, then a choice—that comprise the crucial intervals between the trigger and our eventual behavior. These intervals are so brief we sometimes fail to segregate them from what we regard as our "behavior." But experience and common sense tell us they're real.

When a trigger is pulled we have an impulse to behave a certain way. That's why some of us hear a loud crash behind us and immediately duck our heads to protect ourselves. The more shrewd and alert among us aren't as quick to run for cover. We hear the sound and look around to see what's behind it—in case there's even more to worry about. Same trigger, different responses, one of them automatic and hasty (in a word, impulsive, as in yielding to the first impulse), the other intermediated by pausing, reflecting, and sifting among better options. We are not primitive sea slugs responding with twitchy movement whenever we're poked with a needle. We have brain cells. We can think. We can make any impulse run in place for a brief moment while we choose to obey or ignore it. We make a choice not out of unthinking habit but as evidence of our intelligence and engagement. In other words, we are paying attention.

For example, in 2007 I was a guest on the *Today* show's weekend edition, interviewed by Lester Holt. Guests are warned that the time on camera goes by very fast—a six-minute segment feels like sixty seconds. It's true. My interview went well. I enjoyed myself so much, in fact, that I was stunned when I heard Lester thanking me for being on the program—the customary cue that the segment is over. I couldn't believe it. We'd just started. I had a half dozen additional points to make. Lester's words triggered an impulse in me to say, "No, let's keep going." And, in fact, the words were on the tip of my tongue. But this was national television, with 4 million people watching. I was keyed up, mindful of every word and gesture. In that nanosecond before the foolish words could pass my lips, I paused to reflect on the consequences of doing so. Was I really considering telling the *Today* host that I didn't want the interview to end? Did I want to be the guest who overstayed his welcome? In the end, I took Lester's cue and responded with the customary, "Thank you for having me."

I'm sure anyone watching the segment's final seconds saw

a guest behaving on autopilot. That's what most exchanges of gratitude are—formulaic gestures, neither distinctive nor attention-grabbing. A viewer wouldn't have an inkling of the split-second drama in my head during the interval between Lester Holt's triggering words and the response I finally chose. Though it looked like rote behavior, it was anything but casual or automatic. Even with a trigger as minor as being thanked for showing up, I was weighing my options. I had a choice.

If we're paying attention (and being on national TV will increase anyone's level of awareness), this is how triggers work. The more aware we are, the less likely any trigger, even in the most mundane circumstances, will prompt hasty unthinking behavior that leads to undesirable consequences. Rather than operate on autopilot, we'll slow down time to think it over and make a more considered choice.

We already do this in the big moments. When we go into our first meeting with the company's CEO, we are mindful that every word, every gesture, every question is a trigger. When we're asked for our opinion, we don't say the first thing that comes to mind. We know we've entered a field of land mines where any misstep may have unappealing consequences. We measure our words like a diplomat facing an adversary. Perhaps we've even prepared our answers ahead of time. Either way, we don't yield to impulse. We reflect, choose, then respond.

Paradoxically, the big moments—packed with triggers, stress, raw emotions, high stakes, and thus high potential for disaster—are easy to handle. When successful people know it's showtime, they prepare to put on a show.

It's the little moments that trigger some of our most outsized and unproductive responses: The slow line at the coffee shop, the second cousin who asks why you're still single, the neighbor who doesn't pick up after his dog, the colleague who doesn't remove his sunglasses indoors to talk to you, the guests who show up too early, the passenger in the next seat wearing super-loud headphones, the screaming baby on the plane, the friend who always one-ups your anecdotes, the person standing on the *left* side of the escalator, and so on.

These are life's paper cuts. They happen every day, and they're not going away. They often involve people we'll never see again. Yet they can trigger some of our basest impulses.

Some of us suppress the impulse. Whatever the reason—common sense, fear of confrontation, more urgent things to do—we opt to ignore the triggering annoyance. We disarm the moment. If there are no bullets in the gun, the trigger doesn't matter.

On the other hand, some of us are easily triggered—and can't resist our first impulse. We have to speak up. This is how ugly public scenes begin. These tiny annoyances should trigger bemusement over life's rich tapestry instead of turning us into umbrage-taking characters from a *Seinfeld* episode.

Even more perilous are the small triggering moments with our families and best friends. We feel we can say or do anything with these folks. They know us. They'll forgive us. We don't have to edit ourselves. We can be true to our impulses. That's how our closest relationships often become trigger festivals with consequences that we rarely see in any other part of our lives—the fuming and shouting, the fights and slammed doors, the angry departures and refusals to talk to each other for months, years, decades.

For example, your teenage daughter borrows the car and

two hours later calls to say it's been stolen. She left the keys in the car while she ran into a convenience store for a snack. A low-probability event (the theft) made more probable by a silly mistake (forgetting the keys). As a parent, how do you respond? Your daughter wasn't harmed. She's not in danger or legal peril. She's a victim. At worst, you've lost property. What's your first impulse?

You can get angry. You can do a variation on "I told you so" or "You always do this," reinforcing the message that 1) parent knows best or 2) your daughter is not as smart as she thinks she is. You can be consoling. You can ask, "Do you need a ride home?" You have options.

I don't have the perfect answer. I do know that this phone call is a supercharged triggering moment, even though it is brief and unexpected and in the grand scheme of things, small. The damage is done. It's not a tall tale to entertain your grandkids years from now. But how you respond is important and consequential. Will this unfortunate event trigger more damage in the relationship between parent and child, or will something good come out of it? Will you give in to the perfectly natural impulse to express your scorn, or will you take a breath and make a smarter choice?

Chapter 6

We Are Superior Planners and Inferior Doers

Why don't we become the person we want to be? Why don't we do what we know we should do, or for that matter, what we plan to do?

It's an eternal question, as old as Aristotle. I believe I have a satisfying answer, but to appreciate it requires backtracking to the beginning of my career.

When I was getting my Ph.D. at UCLA in the 1970s, my mentor was a pioneering organizational psychologist named Paul Hersey. Paul's most durable contribution to the field of organizational behavior was a concept he called "situational leadership." He developed it with my friend and hero, Ken Blanchard.

Hersey and Blanchard's premise was that leaders need to adapt their style to fit the performance readiness of their followers. Readiness not only varies by person, it also varies by task. Followers have different levels of motivation and ability for different tasks. For example, Jerry, an outstanding salesman, might have a high readiness level for the task of calling on customers but a low readiness level for completing sales reports. The most effective leaders can vary their leadership style to fit the needs of the situation. Hence, the term *situational leadership*.

Hersey and Blanchard believed that leaders should

- keep track of the shifting levels of "readiness" among their followers,
- stay highly attuned to each situation,
- acknowledge that situations change constantly, and
- fine-tune their leadership style to fit the followers' readiness.

This was "situational leadership." It dissected the relationship between leaders and their followers into four distinct styles:

1. *Directing* is for employees requiring a lot of specific guidance to complete the task. The leader might say, "Chris, here's what I'd like you to do, step by step. And here's when I need it done." It's primarily a one-way conversation, with little input from the employee.
2. *Coaching* is for employees who need more than average guidance to complete the task, but with above-average amounts of two-way dialogue. Coaching is for people who both want and need to learn. The leader might say, "Chris, here's what I'd like you to do," and then ask for input: "What do you think, Chris?"
3. *Supporting* is for employees with the skills to complete the task but who may lack the confidence to do it on

their own. This style features below-average amounts of direction. The leader might say, "Chris, here's the task. How do you think it should be done? Let's talk about it. How can I help you on this one?"

4. *Delegating* is for employees who score high on motivation, ability, and confidence. They know what to do, how to do it, and can do it on their own. The leader might say, "Chris, here's the assignment. You have a great track record. If I can help, just ask. If not, you're on your own."

The four styles are exempt from qualitative judgment. One style is not "better" than another. Each is appropriate to the situation.*

Effective leaders know this intuitively. They know who on their team can be left alone and who needs more direction.

---

*The 1949 film *Twelve O'Clock High* is nearly forgotten now, but it is still much admired in business schools as a step-by-step illustration of situational leadership. Over the years I've had at least ten thousand people watch it in class and then we discuss it. Gregory Peck, playing World War II general Frank Savage, displays all four leadership styles as he remolds a "bad luck" American bomber squadron into fighting trim. A more recent example is *Hoosiers,* based on the Milan, Indiana, high school team that won the 1954 state basketball championship. Gene Hackman plays the new coach who, displaying strict directing style, makes his team relearn the fundamentals. He evolves through the coaching and supporting styles. In the film's climactic scene, he evolves into a more delegating style. With the game tied and his team with the ball, Hackman diagrams a final play in the huddle, using the star player Jimmy Chitwood as a decoy. The players are silent. Hackman asks, "What's the matter?" The team wants their star to take the last shot. The star player looks at Hackman and, overruling the decoy plan, says, "I'll make it." The coach sees that his star has the motivation, ability, and confidence to get the job done. Of course, he does.

Other strong leaders learn it through observation and trial and error. The least effective leaders never get it. They're the ones who tell a talkative subordinate, "You need to be a better listener" and expect that one-time conversation to make a lasting impression. They don't see the irony in telling a bad listener to be a better listener and then being surprised that the subordinate didn't listen.

Situational leadership is a well-known theory that's been applied in training millions of leaders around the world. Because I learned it early in my career from its creators I believe it in my bones. It's one of the big reasons I've made a career out of helping business leaders develop better relationships with their colleagues and subordinates.

Measure Your Need, Choose Your Style

But how does situational leadership explain why we don't become the person we want to be?

What I've realized is that Hersey and Blanchard's situational leadership is a perfect analogue to a hidden dynamic that exists within us when we attempt to change our behavior. It's the same dynamic whether you call it leader and follower, planner and doer, or manager and employee. The terms are interchangeable as far as I'm concerned.

As we go through life making plans to be a better friend, partner, worker, athlete, parent, son, or daughter, inside each of us are two separate personas. There's the leader/planner/manager who plans to change his or her ways. And there's the follower/doer/employee who must execute the plan. We think they are the same because we unwittingly function as one or the other throughout our day. They are both part of who we are. But we are wrong.

In fact, we start each day as a bifurcated individual, one part leader, the other part follower—and as the day progresses, the two grow further apart.

Think back on how you start your day. If you're like most people, you wake up as a leader who has worthy plans for the day. You may even have a to-do list in writing. As you're looking at your to-do list, you're feeling confident and motivated about your day. Why wouldn't you? You have a plan. A plan is a good thing. At that moment, you are functioning as a leader. But later on in the same day, with little to no awareness, you assume a different role. You become the follower, the person who has to execute the leader's wishes.

As the leader, you assume the follower in you will obey each order precisely as you have articulated it. And that your follower self will not be presented with any reasons to fail during the day. (After all, who plans to fail?) You ignore the possibility that the worker in you will be upset by a customer or colleague, or called away to deal with an emergency, or fall behind because a meeting ran over time. The day will go smoothly. Everything will fall into place. Not just this one day, but every day.

Now ask yourself this: *When has your day ever worked out note for note as you planned it?*

As a leader, when have your people followed up precisely as you dictated, in the time frame you outlined, with a result that was as good or better than you expected, and with the attitude you hoped for?

It rarely happens. (The occasions when it does stand out in sharp relief as celebration-worthy exceptions.)

So why would you expect it to happen when you are simultaneously both leader and follower, manager and worker? Why would you expect everything to go smoothly just because you're barking orders at yourself, not someone else?

Whether you're leading other people or leading the follower in you, the obstacles to achieving your goals are the same. You still have to deal with an environment that is more hostile than supportive. You still have to face other people who tempt you away from your objectives. You still have to factor in the high probability of low-probability events. And you still have to consider that as the day goes on and your energy level diminishes, your motivation and self-discipline will flag.

It slowly dawned on me that the precepts of situational leadership might be useful in the context of self-managed adult behavioral change. What if the planner in each of us, like an effective leader with his or her subordinates, could size up the situation at any point during the day and adopt the appropriate management style for the doer in us? It's a simple two-step: measure the need, choose the style.

Many of us already do this kind of self-assessment automatically. When it matters, we have an instinctive sense of how much self-management help we need. Some goals demand little to no direction and oversight. We don't write the goal down, or slot it for a specific time, or ask our assistant to remind us to do it. The planner in us is *delegating* the job to the doer in us—and assuming it will get done.

Other tasks and situations, however, demand a heavier *guiding* hand. For example, in the matter of *showing up for my daughter's wedding,* my need for guidance and self-management is low. I'm not likely to forget time and date, the address, and what to wear. Absent an unforeseen catastrophe, I don't need direction to get me to the church on time. It's so important nothing can distract me from achieving it.

On the other hand, in the matter of *how to behave at the wedding* my need for direction is slightly higher. I say this feelingly because it's what happened at my daughter Kelly's wedding in 2013. Before the rehearsal dinner, she took me aside and gave me my marching orders on what I could say or do and who I had to be especially careful with. "Dad, don't act like you're teaching a class," she said.

I didn't feel abused by Kelly's orders. She correctly assessed my high need for guidance—and I embraced it. (The groom's father later told me his wife had done the same with him.) Even during the long and joyous day of the wedding and reception, I reminded myself of her words by periodically checking in with my wife, Lyda, to ask, "How'm I doing?" This was my interpretation of a participative self-management style.

I apply this situational approach—that how we manage others is how we should manage ourselves—with clients. One of the first occasions was with a client named Rennie, who had taken a big pay cut as a corporate attorney to serve in his state governor's cabinet. Unfortunately, what worked for Rennie as a senior partner at a big law firm with a team of associates at his beck and call wasn't working in a government department where workers and resources were limited. Rennie had a habit of handing out the same assignments to three or four people, thus sowing needless confusion and redundant effort among his staffers.

Rennie wasn't a manipulator. He didn't begin each day planning to confuse and annoy his direct reports. He was a virtuous and principled man, deeply invested in doing good.

Plus, he was aware of his bad habit and wanted to control himself. But the environment of a staff meeting triggered a change in Rennie. He would get excited about a project and want everyone involved—and the overlapping assignments would fly out of his mouth. The calm leader who at the start of the day planned to contain himself was not the eager doer in the meeting. Despite all the good intentions, Rennie became divisive rather than inclusive. He was the follower who couldn't execute his own plan.

I asked myself: What if Rennie the planner learned to adopt a more appropriate management style for Rennie the doer? What if he could be taught a better approach for staff meetings, which triggered the divisive behavior?

I discussed this with Rennie and we agreed that his need for guidance in staff meetings was high. Very high. He couldn't go into meetings *hoping* he'd behave himself. He needed clear instructions available to him at all times. Our solution came in the form of an index card, which Rennie placed in front of himself at every staff meeting. The card said, "Don't confuse your staff. Don't give the same assignment to more than one person." It may sound corny or simplistic, but when the discussion became intense and Rennie was most vulnerable, the card was all the reminder he needed to think before he made an assignment. This is how Rennie's inner planner got in sync with his inner doer.

This is where the analogy between situational leadership in the workplace and in ourselves applies. In order to change his unproductive behavior as a leader of others Rennie first had to change the behavior between the leader and the follower in him. He couldn't automatically rely on a seamless compliance between these two personas. Specific situations—in his case, staff meetings—broke the connection. Once he became mindful of his vulnerability in staff meetings, it wasn't hard to figure out what he had to do. An index card was all the direction and structure Rennie the follower required.

Now let's move beyond the workplace and into a more personal context. Let's use the term *planner* for the part of us that intends to change our behavior and *doer* for the part of us that actually makes change happen. The disconnect is the same: *We are superior planners and inferior doers.*

- The planner-husband who fully intends to be nicer to his wife all day is not the doer-husband who snaps at her that evening because she interrupts him while he's watching *SportsCenter.*
- The executive mom who plans to spend more time with her children is not the doer who misses her daughter's swim meet because of a late-afternoon crisis at the office.
- The would-be good son who plans to call his mother every Sunday without fail is not the doer who misses a couple of Sundays because calling one or two Sundays a month is "good enough."

The examples of our well-meant planning and less-than-stellar doing are as numerous as the people we know and the situations we encounter. Our failure to do what we plan is a certainty like death and taxes.

It's not just environmental intrusions and unpredicted events that upset our plans. It's also our willful discounting of past experience. We make plans that are wholly contradicted by our previous actions. The planner who intends to make a deadline is also the myopic doer who forgets that he has *never* made a deadline in his life. The planner believes this time will be different. The doer extends the streak of missed deadlines.

The yawning gap between planner and doer persists even when conditions for success are practically ideal.

In the spring of 2014 I hosted a dinner for seventeen of my coaching clients at the Four Seasons restaurant in New York. The next day we would all be spending an intense full-day session together to share personal goals. The dinner was the standard pre-session icebreaker where guests get to know one another. I started by asking for a show of hands. I said, "I want everyone here to promise they will not interrupt or say anything judgmental during dinner. Every time you fail it will cost you twenty dollars on the spot." Seventeen hands went up. They all promised to follow the rules. As a further prod, I predicted that all of them would break their promise.

Within ten minutes, I had more than four hundred dollars in twenties piled up at the center of the table. (The money would go to the Nature Conservancy, whose chief executive was also at the table.) A half hour later, the money had doubled. At one point the recently retired CEO of one of the world's biggest companies got up from the table to visit an ATM. He'd run out of cash. Half of the guests were self-made entrepreneurs with net worths in the eight figures. The other half had the words *President* or *CEO* on their business cards. Not an undisciplined slacker in the bunch. Genuinely nice people, too. Plus, they were fully armed with all the tools they needed to keep their promise:

- I gave them a plan.
- They promised to keep it.

- They were at risk of failing only for the three hours at the table—a relatively brief window of time to maintain disciplined behavior.
- There was a financial penalty, which incentivizes good behavior.
- I had warned them that they were likely to fail, reinforcing their awareness of the plan—and in this alpha crowd, motivating them to prove me wrong.
- The required task was not beyond their abilities. All they had to do was avoid making negative comments—in other words, keep their mouths shut.

Yet 16 out of the 17 guests had to reach into their pockets and pull out twenty-dollar bills for the kitty.* They couldn't overcome their environment. The doer in them, swaddled in a convivial atmosphere that tends to loosen tongues, could not keep a promise that the planner in each had made a few minutes earlier.

The boxer-philosopher Mike Tyson said, "Everyone has a plan until they get punched in the face." As we wander through life, what punches us in the face repeatedly is our environment.

---

*The exception was Rennie who, I later learned, raised his hand and then wrote "No interruptions, no judgment" on an index card that he discreetly tucked under his water glass within his line of vision.

Chapter 7

Forecasting the Environment

In San Diego, where I live, I can always identify the neighbors who are fanatical sailors, surfers, or golfers. They're the ones checking their phones for hourly weather updates. That makes sense. San Diego has some of the most reliable weather on the planet, but sometimes it doesn't. So my neighbors use all the tools at their disposal to determine if the wind on the Pacific Ocean will be fresh, the surf will be up, and the golf course will be playable. They are not only aware of the environment, they go out of their way to forecast it.

Few of us shape our days with the obsessive forecasting that avid sailors, surfers, and golfers take for granted. If we did, we wouldn't be blindsided by our environment so often.

Forecasting is what we must do after acknowledging the environment's power over us. It comprises three interconnected stages: anticipation, avoidance, and adjustment.

1. Anticipation

Successful people are not completely oblivious to their environment. In the major moments of our lives, when the outcome really matters and failure is not an option, we are masters of anticipation.

When an ad agency team enters a client's conference room to pitch an account, they've already honed their presentation, researched the client's biases, and rehearsed sharp answers to deflect any pushback. They imagine the positive emotional temperature in the room when they're finished—and then design their pitch to create it.

It's the same with trial attorneys who never ask a question to which they don't know the answer. Their entire line of questioning a witness is based on anticipation.

It's the same with a public official chairing a town meeting on a divisive issue. The official anticipates that some comments will be said in anger, that the exchanges could become inflammatory and personally insulting. In a heated environment, she reminds herself to stay cool and be fair. She may prepare some mollifying remarks. She may even request a police presence.

Likewise with a young man before he asks his girlfriend to marry him. If he follows convention, the gesture is an exercise in extreme anticipation—from the selection of the setting to choosing the right moment to pop the question—all in an effort to elicit the anticipated response from the object of his affection. (Brides often reciprocate with an even greater display of anticipation on their wedding day.)

When our performance has clear and immediate consequences, we rise to the occasion. We create our environment.
We don't let it re-create us.

The problem is that the majority of our day consists of minor
moments, when we're not thinking about the environment or
our behavior because we don't associate the situation with
any consequences. These seemingly benign environments,
ironically, are when we need to be most vigilant. When we're
not anticipating the environment, anything can happen.*

I once thought it would be useful to introduce two of my
clients to each other over dinner. Edgar was an Ivy League-
educated president of a liberal think tank in New York City.
He had the silky diplomatic skills of a man who spent half
his time asking wealthy donors for money. Mike was a gre-
garious, slightly roguish head of an energy company in Okla-
homa. I thought their different backgrounds would make for
an interesting evening. They'd broaden their minds and have
me to thank for it.

Wrong. In my experience, when smart people meeting
for the first time run low on conversation, they turn to pol-
itics. If they're of the same political stripe, they have a jolly
time agreeing on how bad the other side is. If they're opposed
politically, they try to convince the other that he's wrong.
That's what happened at dinner. Edgar was a rabid liberal.
Mike the oilman was a hardened conservative. Things went
well up to the appetizers. But after the friendly talk about

---

*If you've ever made a thoughtless but seemingly innocent comment
to a loved one or colleague that escalated into a World War III argument or irreparably hurt feelings, you know what I'm talking about.

jobs, families, vacation plans, and sports had been dispensed with, they defaulted to current events. It was as if they'd been handed a checklist of hot-button issues—border security, energy policy, gun control, legal marijuana, affirmative action, government spending—so each man could futilely try to change the other's point of view. They spent thirty minutes arguing over secondhand smoke, though neither man was an expert on or even cared about the issue. It was an evening of two strong-minded males expressing their need to win. I was a miserable spectator.

The fault was mine, not theirs. As Samuel Johnson said of a widower remarrying soon after the end of an unhappy marriage, I exhibited "the triumph of hope over experience."

I should have known better. I knew their political differences. I'm the one who placed them across the table from each other with no one else to distract them. In hindsight, I'm convinced their behavior would have been different in an office setting. In that workplace environment, they'd display appropriate workplace behavior. They'd be cordial *and* professional. My big mistake, though, was a failure to anticipate their behavior in the after-hours environment of dinner at a restaurant—when both men considered themselves off-duty, free to say anything because it would have no business repercussions. Proper anticipation would have led to . . .

2. Avoidance

Peter Drucker famously said, "Half the leaders I have met don't need to learn what to do. They need to learn what to stop."

It's no different with our environment. Quite often our smartest response to an environment is avoiding it.

- If we're returning home late at night, we don't take a route through a sketchy high-crime neighborhood.
- If we've given up drinking, we don't hang out at a bar.
- If we're fair-skinned and burn easily in the sun, we skip the beach.
- If we detest our neighbor Todd, we politely turn down his invitations to visit.

We're generally shrewd about avoiding environments that present a physical or emotional risk or are otherwise unpleasant.

On the other hand, we rarely triumph over an environment that is enjoyable. We'd rather continue enjoying it than abandon or avoid it.

Part of the reason is inertia. It takes enormous willpower to stop doing something enjoyable.

A bigger part, though, is our fundamental misunderstanding of the relationship between our environment and temptation. Temptation is the mocking sidekick who shows up in any enjoyable environment, urging us to relax, try a little of this or that, stay a little longer. Temptation can corrupt our values, health, relationships, and careers. Because of our delusional belief that we control our environment, we choose to flirt with temptation rather than walk away. We are constantly testing ourselves against it. And dealing with the shock and distress when we fail.

Sometimes the temptation is as trivial as having a second slice of cheesecake. Other times it's a major-league challenge, like agreeing too quickly to an irresistible deal even when we know we can't deliver on schedule.

I see this thinking all the time among my successful clients. They love a challenge. They award themselves merit points for triumphing over temptation. Avoidance to them is not an achievement. It's the negative option created by passivity. It happens by default.

This impulse to *always engage* rather than *selectively avoid* is one reason I'm called in to coach executives on their behavior.* It's one of the most common behavioral issues among leaders: succumbing to the temptation to exercise power when they would be better off showing restraint.

I had an unusual case with a longtime client named Stan. After years starting and selling companies and running a Fortune 50 corporation, Stan retired at age seventy to serve on a few boards, consult a little, and fulfill his dream of giving away half his fortune via a foundation to support medical re-

---

*I privately refer to this attitude in my clients as the "dramatic narrative fallacy"—the notion that we have to spice up our day by accepting more, if not all, challenges, as if our life resembled a TV drama where the script says we overcome seemingly insurmountable odds rather than avoid them. That's okay for recreational pursuits, like training for a triathlon. But life becomes exhaustingly risky if we apply that attitude to *everything*. Sometimes the better part of valor—and common sense—is saying, "I'll pass." Golfers believe a boring round of golf is a great round of golf. You drive the ball into the fairway, hit your next shot onto the green not too far from the pin, then sink your first putt for birdie or your second putt for par. Then you walk to the next tee and do it again. Do this for eighteen holes and you'll either shoot a personal best or break the course record. Given the choice, golfers will take a dull round of that caliber over a dramatic roller coaster every time.

search. He installed his wife as the foundation's head and his two grown daughters as her lieutenants.

Stan called me, inviting me to sit in on a family meeting at his home in Connecticut. Minutes into the meeting, I could see the problem. Stan's family was ignoring him. He would bark out commands to his wife, a formidably accomplished woman, and she would respond, "I am your wife and the head of the foundation. Don't confuse me with one of your employees." Stan had this exchange more than once and still didn't take the hint. He'd turn to his daughters, one a lawyer, the other a doctor, and order them around. They'd say, "We report to Mom."

This was not Stan's first frustrating meeting with his family. I was there at his invitation to coach him on how to get his wife and kids to listen.

"It's not gonna happen," I said to Stan.

"But I'm the one who paid for everything. They can't shut me out," he said.

"True," I nodded. "But irrelevant. You're making a false equivalency between your career as a CEO and your authority at home. Your family obviously doesn't see it that way. You put them in charge. The foundation is their responsibility. You can't undo that. All you can do is accept that you may be in charge at work but not at home."

The problem, I quickly saw, was "environmental." Holding the meeting in a home environment rather than at the foundation's office confused the situation: was this a business or family matter? It certainly confused Stan, who behaved like an imperious chief executive when he should have been a more inclusive husband and father. I knew Stan to be a classic "people person," an expert at reading the temperature in any room. Yet here with his family, triggered by the environment of his home, he was behaving against his best interests—and unaware of it.

"What would it cost you psychically to exit the situation?" I asked.

"It was my idea," said Stan, persisting in his belief that he still had "ownership" in the foundation.

"Stan, your family is rebelling against your behavior, not you," I said. "Even if you change your ways, who's to say they'd accept it, or you wouldn't revert to the old you? You'd be better off avoiding them."

It took Stan a few minutes to accommodate avoidance as a solution. Worst case, I explained, the fighting with his family would cease immediately. Best case, his wife and daughters might eventually turn to him for advice. But it wouldn't happen until he took himself out of the picture.

I don't usually cite politicians as role models, but they are masters of avoidance. Unlike my high-achieving clients (who can't foresee error-inducing situations because they're neither used to erring nor admitting its possibility), politicians are terrorized by the specter of a career-ending gaffe. So they develop perfect pitch for any environment that might tempt them into making a gaffe. When they refuse to answer a no-win question at a press conference, they're practicing avoidance. When they won't be seen in the same room with a polarizing public figure, they're avoiding. When they abstain from a controversial vote, they're avoiding.

Politicians know this instinctively. Why don't we?

It's a simple equation: *To avoid undesirable behavior, avoid the environments where it is most likely to occur.* If you don't want to be lured into a tantrum by a colleague who gets on your nerves, avoid him. If you don't want to indulge in late-night snacking, don't wander into the kitchen looking for leftovers in the fridge.

3. Adjustment

Of course, there are many moments in life when avoidance is impossible. We have to engage, even if doing so terrifies us (for example, public speaking), or enrages us (for example, visiting our in-laws), or turns us into jerks (for example, conducting business with people we don't respect).

Adjustment, if we're lucky, is the end product of forecasting—but only after we anticipate our environment's impact and eliminate avoidance as an option. Adjustment doesn't happen that often. Most of us continue our errant ways unchecked. We succeed *despite*, not *because of*, falling into the same behavioral traps again and again. Adjustment happens when we're desperate to change, or have an unexpected insight, or are shown the way by another person (such as a friend or coach).

This was the case with a rising tech executive named Sachi, whom I met in Silicon Valley. Sachi was raised in a small village in India without money or advantage. She worked hard and, with great help from her proud parents, was one of the few women to graduate in electrical engineering from the prestigious Indian Institute of Technology in Delhi. After a few years working in Silicon Valley, she received her MBA from Stanford. At thirty she was already at the director level at a top software firm.

Sachi told me about her return visit to her village. She was having dinner with seven of her old friends. One friend asked a seemingly innocent question: "What did you do last week?"

Sachi shared the details of an exciting week. She had flown to Paris for a conference and met with a few icons in her industry. She was leading the development phase for a new product. Her CEO had just told her that she had been tapped for the company's high-potential leadership program. She bubbled over with enthusiasm.

After dinner, everyone said goodbye except Sachi's closest childhood friend, Ranjini. Ranjini was not as wildly successful as Sachi but was advancing steadily in a large Indian company. The others at dinner were faring less well. As Sachi talked about how much she enjoyed the reunion, Ranjini interrupted her to say, "Do you think people want to hear you popping off about Paris and new products and CEOs? When did you become such a show-off?"

Sachi was crushed at first, then defended herself: "They asked me what I did last week. So I told them."

It took her a few sleepless hours that night to realize that she'd completely misread her situation. She wasn't dealing with a group of whiz kids in Silicon Valley. She was dealing with poor people who grew up with her but had never gone as far as she had. In her mind, she was sharing her life. In their minds she was rubbing their noses in it.

She reproached herself for not anticipating this and for behaving so insensitively. But making mistakes is how we learn. She realized that a simple question can trigger a simple response that's appropriate in one environment and completely wrong in another.

On her next trip back, when she met with a group of villagers and was asked about her job, Sachi said, "Mostly techni-cal stuff. There's a lot of travel. That part is tough." And then she turned her considerable charm and attention to ask about their lives.

Sachi did what anyone would do with a heightened aware-ness of the environment. She was adjusting.

Chapter 8

The Wheel of Change

L et's review what we've learned so far.

I've taken the position that there is no harder task for adults than changing our behavior. We are geniuses at coming up with reasons to avoid change. We make excuses. We rationalize. We harbor beliefs that trigger all manner of denial and resistance. As a result, we continually fail at becoming the person we want to be.

One of our greatest instances of denial involves our relationship with our environment. We willfully ignore how profoundly the environment influences our behavior. In fact, the environment is a relentless triggering mechanism that, in an instant, can change us from saint to sinner, optimist to pessimist, model citizen to thug—and make us lose sight of who we're trying to be.

The good news is that the environment is not conducting a cloak-and-dagger operation. It's out in the open, providing constant feedback to us. We're often too distracted to hear what the environment is telling us. But in those moments when we're dialed in and paying attention, the seemingly covert triggers that shape our behavior become apparent.

The not-so-good news is that it's hard to stay alert as we move from one environment to another. Our circumstances change from minute to minute, hour to hour—and we can't always summon the ability or motivation to manage each situation as we would like. We mess up. We take one step forward, two steps back.

Moreover, we have a bifurcated response to the environment in which we display two discrete personas I call "planner" and "doer." The planner who wakes up in the morning with clear plans for the day is not the same person later in the day who has to execute those plans. Basic tools such as anticipating, avoiding, and adjusting to risky environments are a good place to start correcting this conflict between planner and doer in us. But they are Band-Aid solutions to immediate challenges; they don't alter our behavior permanently.

Now that I've outlined our frailties in the face of behavioral change and labeled us abject losers in our ongoing war with the environment, you may rightly ask, *When do we get to the good stuff, the action points spelling out something meaningful to do?*

Not so fast. To understand a problem, you not only have to admit there is a problem; you also have to appreciate all your options. And with behavioral change, we have options.

The graphic tool on the next page is one I've been using with clients for years. It illustrates the interchange of two dimensions we need to sort out before we can become the person we want to be: the Positive to Negative axis tracks the elements that either help us or hold us back. The Change to Keep axis tracks the elements that we determine to change or

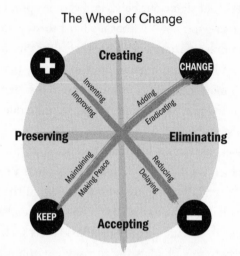

The Wheel of Change

keep in the future. Thus, in pursuing any behavioral change we have four options: change or keep the positive elements, change or keep the negative.

- *Creating* represents the positive elements that we want to create in our future.

- *Preserving* represents the positive elements that we want to keep in the future.

- *Eliminating* represents the negative elements that we want to eliminate in the future.

- *Accepting* represents the negative elements that we need to accept in the future.

These are the choices. Some are more dynamic, glamorous, and fun than others, but they're equal in importance. And three of them are more labor-intensive than we imagine.

1. Creating

Creating is the glamorous poster child of behavioral change. When we imagine ourselves behaving better, we think of it as an exciting process of self-invention. We're creating a "new me." It's appealing and seductive. We can be anyone we choose to be.

The challenge is to do it by choice, not as a bystander. Are we creating ourselves, or wasting the opportunity and being created by external forces instead?

Creating is not an option that comes automatically to even the smartest among us. When I was working with the CEO of a large European company six months before his mandatory retirement, I asked him, "What are you going to do when you leave?"

"I have no idea," he said.*

"If you knew that your company was going to change completely in six months and have new customers, a new identity, would you plan for it?" I asked.

"Of course," he said. "It would be irresponsible not to."

"What's more important? Your company or your life?"

It was a rhetorical question. I was warning him that, stripped of his identity at the top of a sixty-thousand-employee organization, he was vulnerable to boredom, dislocation, depression. I'd seen it before in ex-CEOs who didn't prepare

---

*I hear this so often, I shouldn't be surprised anymore. But I am. It's the main reason I host several "What are you going to do with the rest of your life" get-togethers at my home for my clients. They're not thinking about it. They're not in creation mode.

well for their corporate exit. It would be "irresponsible" if he didn't create a new identity for himself.

I wasn't telling him anything he didn't know. He'd been at the higher levels of corporate life for many years. He'd seen many peers get stranded or lost in so-called retirement. But he hadn't considered applying this insight to himself. He was making the same mistakes the rest of us make.

If we're satisfied with our life—not necessarily happy or delighted that we've exceeded our wildest expectations, just *satisfied*—we yield to inertia. We continue doing what we've always done.

If we're dissatisfied, we may go to the other extreme, falling for any and every idea, never pursuing one idea long enough so that it takes root and actually shapes a recognizably new us. If you know people who flit from one faddish diet to the next—and never lose weight—you know the type. That's chasing, not creating.

As the chart indicates, creating spans a continuum from adding to inventing. Adding one new behavior is usually sufficient for already successful people. In my one-on-one coaching I've never had to help an executive completely overhaul his or her personality. Successful leaders don't behave inappropriately across the board (if they did, they'd be unemployed). But they often behave inappropriately in one or two areas, which colors people's perceptions of everything else they do.

We always have a chance to create better behavior in ourselves—how we treat people, how we respond to our environment, what we permit to trigger our next action. All we need is the impulse to imagine a different us.

2. Preserving

Preserving sounds passive and mundane, but it's a real choice. It requires soul-searching to figure out what serves us well, and discipline to refrain from abandoning it for something new and shiny and not necessarily better.

We don't practice preserving enough. Successful people, by definition, are doing a lot of things correctly, so they have a lot to preserve. But they also have a baseline urge that equates steady advancement with constant improvement. They're geared to fight the status quo, not maintain it. When they face the choice of *being good* or *getting even better*, they instinctively opt for the latter—and risk losing some desirable qualities.

In its sly way, preserving can be transformational. When my friend (and, full disclosure, one of my all-time heroes) Frances Hesselbein, whom *Fortune* magazine called "the best non-profit manager in America," became CEO of the Girl Scouts of America in 1976, her mandate was to transform a hidebound organization with declining membership, a reliance on 120 volunteers for every paid staff member, and an anachronistic image that no longer applied to young girls. The urge to scrap everything and rebuild from the ground up would have been understandable. But Frances, who years earlier had volunteered with Troop 17 of the Girl Scouts in her hometown in Pennsylvania, knew that the organization had a lot worth preserving, not only its signature door-to-door cookie sales but its identity of being a moral guide for young women. She showed her staff and volunteers that it was more important than ever to reach out to girls, given the emerging threats of drugs and teen pregnancy. "Tradition with a future," she called her radical combination of preserving and creating, which inspired the organization with new purpose. In her years as CEO, membership quadrupled and diversity tripled.

A politician once told me, "The most thankless decision I make is the one that prevents something bad from happening, because I can never prove that I prevented something even worse." Preserving is the same. We rarely get credit for *not* messing up a good thing. It's a tactic that looks brilliant only in hindsight—and only to the individual doing the preserving.

So we rarely ask ourselves, "What in my life is worth keeping?" The answer can save us a lot of time and energy. After all, preserving a valuable behavior means one less behavior we have to change.

3. Eliminating

Eliminating is our most liberating, therapeutic action—but we make it reluctantly. Like cleaning out an attic or garage, we never know if we'll regret jettisoning a part of us. Maybe we'll need it in the future. Maybe it's the secret of our success. Maybe we like it too much.

The most significant transformational moment in my career was an act of elimination. It wasn't my idea.

I was in my late thirties and doing well flying around the country giving the same talk about organizational behavior to companies. I was on a lucrative treadmill of preserving, but I needed my mentor Paul Hersey to point out the downside.

"You're too good at what you're doing," Hersey told me. "You're making too much money selling your day rate to companies."

When someone tells me I'm "too good" my brain shifts

into neutral—and I bask in the praise. But Hersey wasn't done with me.

"You're not investing in your future," he said. "You're not researching and writing and coming up with new things to say. You can continue doing what you're doing for a long time. But you'll never become the person you want to be."

For some reason, that last sentence triggered a profound emotion in me. I respected Paul tremendously. And I knew he was right. In Peter Drucker's words, I was "sacrificing the future on the altar of today." I could see my future and it had some dark empty holes in it. I was too busy maintaining a comfortable life. At some point, I'd grow bored or disaffected, but it might happen too late in the game for me to do something about it. Unless I eliminated some of the busywork, I would never create something new for myself.

Despite the immediate cut in pay, that's the moment I stopped chasing my tail for a day rate and decided to follow a different path. I have always been thankful for Paul's advice.

We're all experienced at eliminating the things that hurt us, especially when the benefits of doing so are immediate and certain. We will shed an unreliable friend who causes us grief, stop drinking caffeine because it makes us jittery, quit a stultifying job that ruins our day, stop a habit that might be killing us. When the consequence is extreme distress, we binge on elimination.

The real test is sacrificing something we enjoy doing—say, micromanaging—that's not ostensibly harming our career, that we believe may even be working for us (if not others). In these cases, we may ask ourselves, "What should I eliminate?" And come up with nothing.

4. Accepting

CEOs tend to see three of the four elements in the wheel of change with great clarity when it applies to an organization. (If they can't, they're not CEO for long.) Creating is innovating, taking risks on new ventures, creating new profit centers within the company. Preserving is not losing sight of your core business. Eliminating is shutting down or selling off the businesses that no longer fit.

Accepting is the rare bird in this aviary of change. Businesspeople, reluctant to admit any defeat, can't help equating "acceptance" with "acquiescence." I once sat in on a budget meeting with a CEO and his division heads. It was an energy company, highly regulated and subject to the whims of political and social tides. For five years, the tide had been going against various parts of the company. The vulnerable divisions hit their profit targets with shrewd cost cutting as revenue growth stalled, then shrank—a race-to-the-bottom strategy that never ends well. In the sixth year, the division chiefs showed up again with rosy projections, assuming they could eke out profits with more cutting. Finally, the CEO had heard enough. He dismissively tossed the reports into the center of the conference table and said, "This meeting is over. When we reconvene in a week, I want a new plan from each of you based on one criterion: your business will vanish next year and it's never coming back. I want to see projections that accept what's staring us in the face."

Everyone in the room had access to the same data. But only the CEO read them with dispassionate clarity—and acceptance.

In business we have an abundance of metrics—market share, quality scores, customer feedback—to help us achieve acceptance of a dire situation or the need for change. But our natural impulse is to think wishfully (that is, favor the optimal, discount the negative) rather than realistically.

That impulse is even more egregious in interpersonal relationships. Instead of metrics, we rely on impressions, which are open to wide interpretation. We take in what we *want to hear*, but tune out the displeasing notes that we *need to hear*. When our immediate superior reviews our performance with six trenchant comments, one positive, five negative, our ears naturally give more weight to the positive comment. It's easier to accept good news than bad.

Some people even have trouble accepting a compliment. Have you ever said something nice about a friend's attire, and your friend brushes it off with "Oh this? I haven't worn it in years." The correct response is "Thank you," not attacking your judgment and kindness.

Accepting is most valuable when we are powerless to make a difference. Yet our ineffectuality is precisely the condition we are most loath to accept. It triggers our finest moments of counterproductive behavior.

- If our exquisite logic fails to persuade a colleague or spouse to take our position, we resort to shouting at them, or threatening them, or belittling them, as if that's a more winning approach than accepting that reasonable people can disagree.
- If our spouse calls us out on a minor domestic infraction (for example, leaving the refrigerator door open, being late to pick up the kids, forgetting to buy

milk) and we are 100 percent guilty, we'll dredge up an incident from the past when our spouse was at fault. We extend a pointless argument ad nauseam rather than say, "You're right. I'm sorry."

- If our immediate superior rejects our proposal, we grumble to our direct reports about how shortsighted our manager is.

If we reflect on it, I'd wager our episodes of nonacceptance trigger more bad behavior than the fallout from our creating, preserving, and eliminating combined.

When I work on behavioral change with corporate teams, the wheel of change is one of the first exercises I use. With so many disparate voices on a team of four, six, or sometimes a dozen executives, it's crucial to focus people on simple concepts that simplify the debate. Asking people, "What do we need to eliminate?" fosters agreement more swiftly than asking, "What's wrong?" or "What don't you like about your colleagues?" One form requires people to imagine a positive course of action (even when it involves elimination). The other triggers whining and complaining.

When my client Alicia was promoted to head of human resources at a portfolio company of eight different businesses with a total of more than one hundred thousand employees, she was given a clear mandate to increase her office's corporate stature. At many companies HR is solely an administrative responsibility—HR people are keepers of the employee handbook—with little influence over the company's direction and strategy. Not so at Alicia's company. With so many employees, the CEO knew that the decisions his head of human resources made could make or break the organization. The

CEO told Alicia he was giving her a "seat at the table." Her job was as important as head of sales or chief operating officer. He was counting on her not to waste the opportunity.

I spent two intensive days with Alicia and her team as they developed their new "seat at the table" strategy. Using the wheel of change as her template, Alicia told the team they only had to make four decisions: choose one thing to create, preserve, eliminate, and accept. Here's what they came up with:

Creating: To ensure a smarter workforce across the company, particularly in their high-tech portfolio, the team focused on upgrading hiring standards. The new strategy would center on more aggressive recruiting at benchmark companies and top-tier universities.

Preserving: The team spent nearly all day debating this. Everyone had a different answer to the tough question, "What's worth keeping?" Eventually the group settled on a cultural issue. The division had always been a tight and cordial operation. Everyone talked freely with one another. There was little to no infighting. People would pitch in without being asked. The team said, "Let's not lose that feeling, whatever we do." It was a touching moment. Until the team made the choice, I don't think they appreciated the uniquely pleasant environment they had created for themselves.

Eliminating: This was Alicia's suggestion. If we're going to be spending more time promoting the company and traveling to colleges and conferences, that means less office time for the senior team. "We can't be more strategic if we're still administrating," she told the group.

They agreed to delegate more of the "old work" to sub-ordinates. They even clocked their goal: 30 percent fewer hours per team member on paperwork.

Accepting: Improving the company's labor force wouldn't happen overnight—or even in a year or two. They were playing a long game. And it wasn't guaranteed that even if they did their job brilliantly they would get the proper credit for it. The line executives would think all gains were their doing. This was what they shrewdly came to accept: how long change takes and who gets the glory.

That's the simple beauty of the wheel. When we bluntly challenge ourselves to figure out what we can change and what we can't, what to lose and what to keep, we often surprise ourselves with the bold simplicity of our answers.

The wheel is equally useful one-on-one. Even if we're alone in a dark and quiet room, intent on contemplating our future, we're still being distracted by the competing voices mumbling and shouting inside our heads. Posing big-picture questions to ourselves crowds out the distracting voices and shuffles the niggling issues and daily nuisances that upset us to the back of the line, where they belong.

There are no wrong or right answers here—as long as they're honest. I recall my client Steve, a financial executive working in Manhattan but living across the Hudson River in New Jersey, answering this way:

- Creating: "A shorter commute to work."
- Preserving: "The sanctity of my family."
- Eliminating: "My current commute to work."
- Accepting: "I'll never get better at golf."

Commuting, family, and golf? That was a trio I hadn't heard before. I thought Steve was being flip (although clearly he had issues with commuting). But as we discussed it, the rigor and integrity in his answers emerged—as well as the trigger to action.

Yes, Steve hated the three hours a day he spent commuting between his suburban New Jersey home and his downtown Manhattan office. It ate into how much time he could spend with his wife and three children. His passion for golf was one reason he had settled in the suburbs; that's where the courses were. But his answers revealed a shift in priorities, and they were more closely interconnected than I had assumed.

Admitting golf's diminished importance in his life—and accepting it—meant there was no reason to stay in the suburbs. He was free to return to Manhattan, where he could actually walk to work, thus creating a shorter commute, eliminating his misery, and not only preserving but increasing his time with his family. So he sold his big house, moved his family into a place ten minutes from his office, and started showing up at home most nights in time for dinner. He still had behavioral issues at work that we needed to address, but his life's biggest headache had vanished.

Good things happen when we ask ourselves what we need to create, preserve, eliminate, and accept—a test I suspect few of us ever self-administer. Discovering what really matters is a gift, not a burden. Accept it and see.

| | |

In examining why we don't become the person we want to be, I realize that I've run through a laundry list of negative

choices that make us sound like closed-minded drones resisting any opportunity to change. That's okay. Negatives are inevitable when we address why we *don't* do something.

But there's hope. Nadeem defused an imagined enemy by
altering his behavior in public forums. Rennie became a better manager by carrying an index card. Stan reduced family
friction by avoiding family meetings.

These behavioral transformations didn't happen overnight.
Nadeem needed eighteen months to get the nod from his colleagues. Rennie still carries an index card to meetings. Stan
complained for months about being shut out of "his" foundation before he could serenely accept his new family landscape.

It's true they had the benefit of an outside agency—namely
me—pointing out the environment's malign impact on their
behavior. But that kind of insight, which explains why we act
the way we do, can take us only so far. It illuminates our past
more than the way forward.

Executing the change we hold as a concrete image in
our mind is a process. It requires vigilance and diligent self-
monitoring. It demands a devotion to rote repetition that we
might initially dismiss as simplistic and undignified, even
beneath us. More than anything, the process resuscitates an
instinct that's been drilled into us as tiny children but slowly
dissipates as we learn to enjoy success and fear failure—the
importance of trying.

Part Two

Try

Chapter 9

The Power of Active Questions

In my coaching I have only a handful of "magic moves."

Apologizing is a magic move. Only the hardest of hearts will fail to forgive a person who admits they were wrong. Apology is where behavioral change begins.

Asking for help is a magic move. Few people will refuse your sincere plea for help. Asking for help sustains the change process, keeps it moving forward.

Optimism—not only feeling it inside but showing it on the outside—is a magic move. People are automatically drawn to the confident individual who believes everything will work out. They want to be led by this person. They'll work overtime to help this person succeed. Optimism almost makes the change process a self-fulfilling prophecy.

What makes these gestures magical is how effectively they trigger decent behavior in *other* people and how easy they are to do.

This chapter introduces a fourth magic move: asking active questions. Like apologizing or asking for help, it's easy to do.

But it's a different kind of triggering mechanism. Its objective is to alter our behavior, not the behavior of others. But that doesn't make it less magical. The act of self-questioning—so simple, so misunderstood, so infrequently pursued—changes everything.

| | |

I learned about active questions from my daughter, Kelly Goldsmith, who has a Ph.D. from Yale in behavioral marketing and teaches at Northwestern's Kellogg School of Management.

Kelly and I were discussing one of the eternal mysteries in my field—namely, the poor return from American companies' $10 billion investment in training programs to boost employee engagement.

Part of the problem, my daughter patiently explained, is that despite the massive spending on training, companies may end up doing things that stifle rather than promote engagement. It starts with how companies ask questions about employee engagement. The standard practice in almost all organizational surveys on the subject is to rely on what Kelly calls *passive* questions—questions that describe a static condition. "Do you have clear goals?" is an example of a passive question. It's passive because it can cause people to think of what is being done to them rather than what they are doing for themselves.

When people are asked passive questions they almost invariably provide "environmental" answers. Thus, if an employee answers "no" when asked, "Do you have clear goals?" the reasons are attributed to external factors such as "My manager can't make up his mind" or "The company changes strategy every month." The employee seldom looks within to take responsibility and say, "It's my fault." Blame is assigned elsewhere. The passive construction of "Do you have clear goals?" begets a passive explanation ("My manager doesn't set clear goals").

The result, argued Kelly, is that when companies take the natural next step and ask for positive suggestions about making changes, the employees' answers once again focus exclusively on the environment, not the individual. "Managers need to be trained in goal setting" or "Our executives need to be more effective in communicating our vision" are typical responses. The company is essentially asking, "What are we doing wrong?"—and the employees are more than willing to oblige with a laundry list of the company's mistakes.

There is nothing inherently evil or bad about passive questions. They can be a very useful tool for helping companies know what they can do to improve. On the other hand, they can produce a very negative unintended consequence. When asked exclusively, passive questions can be the natural enemy of taking personal responsibility and demonstrating accountability. They can give people the unearned permission to pass the buck to anyone and anything but themselves.

Active questions are the alternative to passive questions. There's a difference between "Do you have clear goals?" and "Did you do your best to set clear goals for yourself?" The former is trying to determine the employee's state of mind; the latter challenges the employee to describe or defend a course of action. Kelly was pointing out that passive questions were almost always being asked while active questions were being ignored.

My Brief History with Engagement

To the untrained eye this was a geeky discussion about semantics between a father and daughter who are overinvested in the intricacies of organizational behavior.

But this was a watershed moment for me. We were talking about employee engagement, a cherished and loaded concept among human resources professionals, who happen to be one of my major client constituencies.

In management circles, engagement is one of those mystically idealized conditions for employees, the equivalent of an athlete being "in the zone" or an artist being in a state of creative "flow." To human resources professionals, employee engagement is not quite the naïve vision of "Whistle While You Work" in Disney's *Snow White and the Seven Dwarfs*—but it's close.

Like "full employment" or world peace, however, employee engagement is also elusive and misunderstood. I have spent years thinking about it and discussing it with professionals. Yet I too have had a checkered history with the concept. Why is engagement so hard to instill in some people, so easy in others?

My puzzlement came to a head when I was invited to speak about coaching at a meeting of human resources executives. The presenters before me, chief HR officers from three leading corporations, were demonstrating why employee engagement is a major variable in the success of an organization. The next described the key drivers of engagement, which included laudable ambitions such as:

- Delivering fair pay and benefits
- Providing the right tools and resources
- Creating a learning environment that encouraged open communication
- Providing variety and challenge in work assignments
- Developing leaders who delegated well, nurtured their direct reports, provided recognition and timely feedback, and built interpersonal relationships.

It all made sense. Who could argue that committed employees willing to go the "extra mile" for their companies wouldn't be more productive than disengaged employees who don't care? Who would take the position that underpaying people and denying them the right tools to do their job was a great way to *increase* engagement?

Then the HR chiefs noted that engagement was near an all-time low! (Gallup research in 2011 showed almost no improvement—with 71 percent of Americans saying that they are "disengaged" or "actively disengaged" in their work.*) They didn't have an explanation for this disconnect and the poor return on investment.

This was news to me at the time. It didn't add up that after all the corporate investment in training, engagement wasn't improving.

But it shouldn't have been a shock. I saw supporting evidence nearly every time I took my seat on a plane. On a typical three-hour flight, some flight attendants are positive, motivated,

---

*Nikki Blacksmith and Jim Harter, "Majority of American Workers Not Engaged in Their Jobs," *Gallup Wellbeing*, November 2011.

upbeat, and enthusiastic. They are models of employee engagement. Other attendants are negative, demotivated, downbeat, and miserable. They are "actively disengaged."

Why the difference? The environment for both attendants is identical—same plane, same customers, same pay, same hours, even the same training—and yet they are demonstrating massively divergent levels of engagement.

I started conducting my own private engagement tests at airline counters and club lounges. Whenever I was asked to show my American Airlines frequent flyer card, which at 11 million miles makes me one of the airline's more loyal customers, I noted the employee's response. It's not a distinctive card (not like the sleek black matte card George Clooney receives when he reaches 10 million miles in *Up in the Air*), so I make sure it gets noticed by asking airline employees, "Have you ever seen one of these before?" In theory a fully engaged airline employee would see my impressive mileage and treat me like royalty—if only because I have showered the company with my patronage and cash. But given the engagement gap I'd experienced among the airline's in-flight employees, I didn't have very high expectations for the people on the ground.

In my experience, fully engaged employees are positive and proactive about their relationship to the job. They not only feel good about what they're doing; they don't mind showing off their enthusiasm to the world. Using those qualities—positive versus negative, proactive versus passive—I tracked the responses to my 11 million miles card to distinguish four levels of engagement:

Committed: The proactively positive employees would examine the card as if they'd never seen it before, and say some

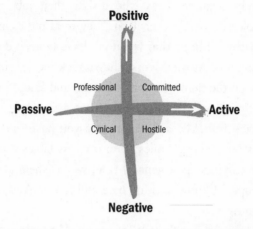

variation on "Hey, this is cool." Some would call over another employee to check out the card. They'd all thank me for my loyalty—and they meant it. Even though we were in the middle of a quickly forgotten exchange—it didn't rise to the level of a transaction, certainly not a relationship—and would not see each other again, the employees made me feel great. That's engagement.

Professional: Then there are the passively positive responses, best expressed by the woman behind the desk in Dallas who offered the sincere pleasantry, "We appreciate your loyalty, sir." That's okay. She made me feel appreciated. She was being a professional.

Cynical: The most common response I get is the passively negative tone of "That's nice, sir." Or "That's interesting." Bored with their job and indifferent to customers, these employees opt for the passive-aggressiveness of being superficially engaged with what they're doing but conveying through their tone of voice that they really don't care.

Hostile: At the bottom of the engagement barrel are the

proactively negative types who dislike their jobs and can barely tolerate me. At their best, they treat me as an object of sympathy ("I hope that you don't have to keep doing this much longer"). At their worst they attack me for simply existing, as in the man who took my card and said, "I'm really tired of you people who fly all the time and expect to get so much back from the airline because you have *miles*." (The way he stretched out "miles" into three syllables was particularly gratifying. As a general rule, when I hear the words "you people" I know nothing nice will follow. And he didn't disappoint.)

Whenever I meet "hostile" or "cynical" people in a service sector job, two questions come to mind:

- What genius hired you for a customer-facing position?
- What happened to you?

Answering the first question is at the core of my professional life. After that meeting, I significantly increased my exhortations to companies on the importance of follow-up *after* they train their employees. It's one of my signature themes: *People don't get better without follow-up. So let's get better at following up with our people.*

Putting Active Questions to the Test

My daughter made me realize that I was still too focused on the company. The fact that I was wondering who hired these people and who put them in the front lines of customer service was a good indicator that I was still holding the employer, not the employee, solely responsible for creating engaged workers. By stressing better follow-up, I was merely increasing the company's burden, asking them to be more thorough in documenting their employees' failures.

There was nothing wrong with my message, but I was ignoring half of the equation: the employee's responsibility for his or her behavior. The difference was not what the company was doing to engage the flight attendants. The difference was what the flight attendants were doing to engage themselves!

This was such a breakthrough for me that I initiated a controlled study with Kelly to test the effectiveness of active questions with employees who undergo training. The theory was that different phrasing of the follow-up questions would have a measurable effect because active questions focus respondents on what they can do to make a positive difference in the world rather than what the world can do to make a positive difference for them. (John F. Kennedy must have known this when he crafted one of the more memorable calls to action in American history: "Ask not what your country can do for you, ask what you can do for your country.")

In the first study, we used three different groups. The first group was a control group that received no training and was asked "before and after" questions on happiness, meaning, building positive relationships, and engagement.

The second group went to a two-hour training session about "engaging yourself" at work and home. This training was followed up every day (for ten working days) with passive questions:

1. How happy were you today?
2. How meaningful was your day?

3. How positive were your relationships with people?
4. How engaged were you?

The third group went to the same two-hour training session. Their training was followed up every day (for ten working days) with active questions:

1. Did you do your best to be happy?
2. Did you do your best to find meaning?
3. Did you do your best to build positive relationships with people?
4. Did you do your best to be fully engaged?

At the end of two weeks, the participants in each of the three groups were asked to rate themselves on increased happiness, meaning, positive relationships, and engagement.

The results were amazingly consistent. The control group showed little change (as control groups are wont to do). The passive questions group reported positive improvement in all four areas. The active questions group doubled that improvement on every item! Active questions were twice as effective at delivering training's desired benefits to employees. While any follow-up was shown to be superior to no follow-up, a simple tweak in the language of follow-up—focusing on what the individual can control—makes a significant difference.

Chapter 10

The Engaging Questions

One study never answers all our questions. To the contrary, it only makes us hungrier for more answers. So we initiated a second ongoing study, this time with the steady stream of participants in my leadership seminars, in which people answered six active questions every day for ten working days. I "reverse-engineered" the questions based on my experience and the literature on the factors that make employees feel engaged. Here are the six Engaging Questions I settled on—and why.

1. Did I do my best to set clear goals today?

Employees who have clear goals report greater engagement than employees who don't. No surprise. If you don't have clear goals and ask yourself, "Am I fully engaged?" the obvious follow-up is "Engaged to do what?" This is true within big organizations as well as for individuals. No clear goals, no engagement. After the 2008 financial crisis I worked with executives at a bank that had gone through three "revolving door" CEOs in three years. The organization was direction-less, and it showed in the disintegrating engagement scores of the senior management. The lowest scores were attached to the question "Do I have clear goals?" Tweaking the question into active form made an immediate difference. Executives demoralized by their leaders' fecklessness became dramatically more engaged after they started setting their own direction for the day instead of futilely waiting to receive it from someone else.

2. Did I do my best to make progress toward my goals today?

Teresa Amabile, in her scrupulous research and in *The Progress Principle*, has shown that employees who have a sense of "making progress" are more engaged than those who don't. We don't just need specific targets; we need to see ourselves nearing, not receding from, the target. Anything less is frustrating and dispiriting. Imagine how you'd feel if you chose a goal and instead of getting better at it, you got worse. How engaged would you be? Progress makes any of our accomplishments more meaningful.

3. Did I do my best to find meaning today?

At this late date, I don't think we have to strenuously argue that finding meaning and purpose improves our lives. I defer here to Viktor Frankl's 1946 classic, *Man's Search for Meaning*. Frankl, an Auschwitz survivor, describes how the struggle to find meaning—the struggle, not the result—can protect us in even the most unimaginable environments. It's up to us, not an outside agency like our company, to provide meaning.

This question challenges us to be creative in finding meaning in whatever we are doing.

4. Did I do my best to be happy today?

People still debate if happiness is a factor in employee engagement. I think that because happiness goes hand in hand with meaning, you need both. When employees report that they are happy but their work is not meaningful, they feel empty—as if they're squandering their lives by merely amusing themselves. On the other hand, when employees regard their work as meaningful but are not happy, they feel like martyrs (and have little desire to stay in such an environment). As Daniel Gilbert shows in *Stumbling on Happiness*, we are lousy at predicting what will make us happy. We think our source of happiness is "out there" (in our job, in more money, in a better environment) but we usually find it "in here"—when we quit waiting for someone or something else to bring us joy and take responsibility for locating it ourselves. We find happiness where we are.

5. Did I do my best to build positive relationships today?

The Gallup company asked employees, "Do you have a best friend at work?" and found the answers directly related to engagement. By flipping the question from passive to active, we're reminded to continue growing our positive relationships, even create new ones, instead of judging our existing relationships. One of the best ways to "have a best friend" is to "be a best friend."

6. Did I do my best to be fully engaged today?

This gets to the head-spinning core of the Engaging Questions: *To increase our level of engagement, we must ask ourselves if we're doing our best to be engaged.* A runner is more likely to run faster in a race by running faster when she trains—and timing herself. Likewise, an employee will be more engaged at work if she consciously tries to be more engaged—and rigorously measures her effort. It's a self-fulfilling dynamic: the act of measuring our engagement elevates our commitment to being engaged—and reminds us that we're personally responsible for our own engagement.

| | |

There are six questions my class attendees voluntarily consider. After ten days we follow up and essentially ask, "How'd you do? Did you improve?" So far we have conducted 79 studies with 2,537 participants. The results have been incredibly positive.

- 37% of participants reported improvement in all six areas.
- 65% improved on at least four items.
- 89% improved on at least one item.
- 11% didn't change on any items.
- 0.4% got worse on at least one item (go figure!).

Given people's demonstrable reluctance to change at all, this study shows that active self-questioning can trigger a new way of interacting with our world. Active questions reveal where we are trying and where we are giving up. In doing so, they sharpen our sense of what we can actually change. We gain a sense of control and responsibility instead of victimhood.

Testing, Testing on Me

As I considered the distinction between *Do you have clear goals?* and *Did you do your best to set clear goals for yourself?* it hit me that I'd been making the same passive-versus-active error in my own life.

For years I've followed a nightly follow-up routine that I call Daily Questions, in which I have someone call me wherever I am in the world and listen while I answer a specific set of questions that I have written for myself. Every day. For the longest time there were thirteen questions, many focused on my physical well-being, because if you don't have your health . . . well, you know the rest. The first question was always "How happy was I today?" (because that's important to me), followed by questions like:

- How meaningful was my day?
- How much do I weigh?
- Did I say or do something nice for Lyda?

And so on. The nightly specter of honestly answering these questions kept me focused on my goal of being a happier and healthier individual. For more than a decade it was the one constant of self-regulated discipline in my otherwise chaotic 180-days-a year-on-the-road life. (I'm not boasting that I do this test; I'm confessing how much discipline I lack.)

If earlier in the day I convinced a client to take our session outside for a long walk, I reported the number of minutes spent walking. If I stayed up late and woke up early, I reported my paltry sleep total. If I forgot to check in with Lyda that day, the answer to the last question was a flat "no." The phone call never took longer than two minutes.

Studying my list of questions in light of Kelly's active/passive distinction, I realized many were phrased poorly, perhaps too passively. They weren't inspiring or motivational. They didn't trigger extraordinary effort out of me. They merely asked me to gauge how I had performed that day on my goals. If I scored poorly on watching TV, there was no self-recrimination or guilt attached to my answer, nothing to make me feel that I was slacking or letting myself down. I could do better the next day. Like most people who answer passive questions, I considered my mistakes more as a function of my environment than myself.

As an experiment, I tweaked the questions using Kelly's "Did I do my best to" formulation.

- Did I do my best to be happy?
- Did I do my best to find meaning?
- Did I do my best to have a healthy diet?
- Did I do my best to be a good husband?

Suddenly, I wasn't being asked how well I performed but rather how much I tried. The distinction was meaningful to me because in my original formulation, if I wasn't happy or I ignored Lyda, I could always blame it on some factor outside myself. I could tell myself I wasn't happy because the airline kept me on the tarmac for three hours (in other words, the airline was responsible for my happiness). Or I overate because a client took me to his favorite barbecue joint, where the food was abundant, caloric, and irresistible (in other words, my client—or was it the restaurant?—was responsible for controlling my appetite).

Adding the words "did I do my best" added the element of *trying* into the equation. It injected personal ownership and responsibility into my question-and-answer process. After a few weeks using this checklist, I noticed an unintended consequence. Active questions themselves didn't merely elicit an answer. They created a different level of engagement with my goals. To give an accurate accounting of my effort, I couldn't simply answer yes or no or "30 minutes." I had to rethink how I phrased my answers. For one thing, I had to measure my effort. And to make it meaningful—that is, to see if I was trending positively, actually making progress—I had to measure on a relative scale, comparing the most recent day's effort with previous days. I chose to grade myself on a 1-to-10 scale, with 10 being the best score. If I scored low on *trying to be happy*, I had only myself to blame. We may not hit our goals every time, but there's no excuse for not trying. Anyone can try.

When I asked myself, "Did I say or do something nice for Lyda?", I could call in a few minutes, say "I love you," and declare victory. When I asked myself, "Did I do my best to be a good husband?", I learned that I had set the bar much higher for myself.

This "active" process will help anyone get better at almost anything. It only takes a couple of minutes a day. But be warned: it is tough to face the reality of our own behavior—and our own level of effort—every day.

Since then I've gone through many permutations of my Daily Questions. The list isn't working if it isn't changing along the way—if I'm not getting better on some issues and adding new ones to tackle. Here's my current list of twenty-two "Did I do my best?" questions that I review every day:

DAILY QUESTIONS				Days				
Did I do my best to: (1–10 scale)	**1**	**2**	**3**	**4**	**5**	**6**	**7**	Weekly average
Set clear goals?	10	9	10	10	7	9	4	**8.43**
Make progress toward goal achievement?	8	10	10	9	8	9	6	**8.57**
Find meaning?	7	9	10	9	9	9	6	**8.43**
Be happy?	8	10	9	8	10	9	9	**9.00**
Build positive relationships?	4	9	10	9	9	10	5	**8.00**
Be fully engaged?	6	10	10	9	8	9	6	**8.29**
Learn something new?	8	3	2	3	9	3	9	**5.29**
Develop new material?	10	0	0	1	7	2	8	**4.00**
Preserve all client relationships?	10	10	10	10	10	10	10	**10.00**
Be grateful for what you have?	10	10	8	10	7	10	9	**9.14**
Avoid angry or destructive comments about others?	8	10	7	9	10	10	10	**9.14**
Forgive yourself and others for perceived mistakes?	10	10	10	10	6	10	8	**9.14**
Avoid trying to prove you're right when it's not worth it?	10	4	6	4	10	9	10	**7.57**
Not waste energy on what you cannot change?	9	8	6	8	10	9	10	**8.57**
Exercise?	8	10	10	10	10	3	8	**8.43**
Meditate?	1	9	10	9	8	8	8	**6.14**
Get a good night's sleep?	10	8	10	10	10	10	10	**9.71**
Have a healthy diet?	10	10	2	4	4	7	3	**5.71**
Say or do something nice for Lyda?	8	8	8	10	8	5	8	**7.86**
Say or do something nice for Bryan?	8	8	8	8	8	8	0	**6.90**
Say or do something nice for Kelly?	5	5	10	8	8	5	0	**5.90**
Say or do something nice for Reid?	0	0	0	0	5	0	0	**0.71**

As you can see, my first six questions are the Engaging Questions that I suggest for everyone. My next eight questions revolve around cornerstone concepts in the wheel of change, where I'm either creating, preserving, eliminating, or accepting. For example, learning something new or producing new editorial content is creating. Expressing gratitude is preserving. Avoiding angry comments is eliminating, and so is avoiding proving I'm right when it's not worth it. Making peace with what I cannot change and forgiving myself is accepting. And the remaining questions are about my family and my health.

There's no correct number of questions. The number is a personal choice, a function of how many issues you want to work on. Some of my clients have only three or four questions to go through each night. My list is twenty-two questions deep because I need a lot of help (obviously) but also because I've been doing this a long time. I've had years to deal with some of the broad interpersonal issues that seem like obvious targets for successful people just starting out with Daily Questions—for example, suppressing the need to win at all times or being more collaborative. I've "conquered" these issues, at least to the point that they're no longer overriding issues worthy of my Daily Questions list.

The week I'm covering in the spreadsheet above is typical for me outside the United States. I traveled from New York to Rome, then Barcelona, then Madrid, then Zurich, and ended with boarding a flight to Djakarta via Singapore. I gave lengthy presentations in each of the four European cities. I had some travel frustrations—a driver who didn't show up (which I could have used as an excuse to get angry). I had some good nights of sleep and some not-so-good (which I could have blamed on the changing time zones in my schedule). I had challenges with my diet, since Rome and Madrid have tempting dining scenes (which I could have used as an excuse to eat too much). I totally enjoyed the time I was standing up in front of people and making a presentation. I spent a lot of time on emails and minor distractions. I didn't get as much writing done as I hoped. All of these outcomes are there for me to reflect on each night as I put in my scores. The net reflection on this particular week: *I need to be a better father-in-law. (My son-in-law Reid is a great guy.) My schedule is a little crazy for a sixty-five-year-old man. I want to continue doing what I'm doing, but maybe slow down a bit. (We'll see. If I don't add this goal to my Daily Questions, I probably don't mean it.)*

The point is, your Daily Questions should reflect your objectives. They're not meant to be shared in public (unless you're writing a book on the subject), meaning they're not designed to be judged. You're not constructing your list to impress anyone. It's your list, your life. I score my "Did I do my best" questions on a simple 1 to 10 scale. You can use whatever works for you. Your only considerations should be:

- Are these items important in my life?
- Will success on these items help me become the person that I want to be?

A Distinction with a Difference

Active questions are not a distinction without a difference. Professional pollsters have always known that *how* questions are posed to interview subjects significantly influences the polling results. (For example, there's a difference between asking if I agree or disagree with the statement, "The best way to ensure peace is through military strength" and asking me to choose between "The best way to ensure peace is through military strength" and "Diplomacy is the best way to ensure peace." The military option is far less popular when people are also given the diplomacy option.)

That's what makes *active* questions a magic move. Injecting the phrase "Did I do my best to . . ." triggers trying.

Trying not only changes our behavior but how we interpret and react to that behavior. Trying is more than a semantic tweak to our standard list of goals. It delivers some unexpected emotional wallops that inspire change or knock us out of the game completely.

Imagine the Daily Questions you'd want on your behavioral change list. If you're like most people, the objectives would fall into a predictable set of broad categories: health, family, relationships, money, enlightenment, and discipline.

There would be a goal or two about intimate personal relationships (being nicer to your partner, more patient with your kids); a couple of diet and fitness goals (reduce sugar consumption, sign up for yoga, floss daily); and a time management goal (get to bed before midnight, limit TV watching to three hours a day).

There would be something involving your behavior at work (asking for help, expanding your contacts, looking for a new job) as well as something more specifically careerist (start blogging, join a professional group, write articles for trade publications).

There would be something involving intellectual stimulation (reading *Middlemarch*, taking an art class, learning Mandarin Chinese) and stopping an undesirable personal habit (biting your nails, saying "You know" too often, throwing clothes on the floor).

And, since we like clear short-term targets, there would be something very specific to achieve in the near future, as trivial as completing an errand or as mind-clearing as redecorating a room.

Go ahead. List the goals on a chart so you can score them at the end of each day. Where appropriate make sure you begin each question with "Did I do my best to . . ." Now study the list and rate your chances of doing well over the next thirty days. If you're like most people—and 90 percent of all people rate themselves above average—you will give yourself a better than 50 percent chance of hitting your targets on all your goals.

At the start of any self-improvement project, when our confidence is high, that's a reasonable assumption. But in a world where we are superior planners and inferior doers, it rarely works out that way.

When I go through this Daily Questions exercise in classes, I hit people with one of my most confident predictions. "Within two weeks," I announce, "half of you will give up and stop answering the Daily Questions."

Then I explain that it's not just that they'll slack off on a few of their goals. They'll give up keeping score altogether. They'll abandon the entire process. That's human nature, I say. In every group, not everyone can get A's, even if people are scoring themselves. Some people will try harder than others, creating a hierarchy of effort. I am confident in my prediction because I have seen it happen so often. It is incredibly difficult for any of us to look in the mirror every day and face the reality that we didn't even try to do what we claimed was most important in our lives.

Even the most ardent practitioners of checklists and Daily Questions—high-profile believers in the concept—are not immune to this kind of pain. When the Boston surgeon and author Atul Gawande published his book *The Checklist Manifesto* in 2011, we spoke on the phone about my Daily Questions. He was intrigued by the notion and said he would adapt questions to his daily routine.

A few months later when I checked in with him, he described how the questions changed his life. Although he was healthy and in his forties, he had a wife and two sons who depended on him. It bothered him that he didn't have life insurance to protect his family. So he added the following to his daily list of questions: *Are you updated on your life insurance?* It wasn't much of a behavioral goal, more like a specific chore that he could do once and erase from his list. And yet . . .

For fourteen consecutive days, he answered the life insurance question with a "no."

As Dr. Gawande stared at the dispiriting string of nos, the irony wasn't lost on him that he saved strangers' lives every day yet he couldn't master the simple task of purchasing life insurance to protect the people he loved most. He was failing a test that he'd written.

But irony doesn't trigger action. The accumulated nos triggered an intense emotion, Gawande told me. He was embarrassed that he had failed to complete such a simple task that delivered a cherished benefit. The next day he bought life insurance.

That's the secret power of daily self-questioning. If we fall short on our goals eventually we either abandon the questions or push ourselves into action. We feel ashamed or embarrassed because we wrote the questions, knew the answers, and still failed the test. When the questions begin with "Did I do my best to . . ." the feeling is even worse. We have to admit that we didn't even try to do what we know we should have done.

Chapter 11

Daily Questions in Action

For Emily R. the trigger was the one-day employee discount at Whole Foods. Forty percent off everything in the store—even the fresh vegetables. Emily had just graduated from the Culinary Institute of America and landed her first job at the supermarket chain's Charlestown branch, a few miles north of downtown Boston.

Emily was twenty-six years old. For most of her life, she'd had a weight problem. She ate poorly and mindlessly, and the problem only got worse when she committed to a career in the culinary arts. She was always cooking, testing recipes, thinking about food. She was obese, at least a hundred pounds over her desired weight.

But who can resist a 40 percent off sale, she thought. As she looked around the market, she considered loading up on the fresh vegetables—the cauliflower and peppers and broccoli and tomatoes and artichokes. She could prepare some healthy meals, give a gentle nudge to doing something about her eating habits and weight, maybe begin a diet—although she'd stopped counting how many times she'd taken that route and failed.

She was also intrigued by the store's shiny new juice bar—the noisy machines surrounded by piles of carrots, kale, celery, cucumbers, and apples and the busy associates grinding out juice drinks all day. It was one of the store's most popular departments. She'd had friends who'd lost weight rapidly on weeklong juice fasts and so-called detoxes. Maybe she could learn more from the juice bar manager. Either way, she was loading up on vegetables.

The manager, heavily tattooed and evangelical about juicing, answered Emily's questions, then made an offer Emily couldn't refuse. "If you buy the vegetables," he said, "I'll give you a juicing machine for free." Emily arrived home that evening with a shopping bag of produce, a chrome Omega juicing machine, and a juicing video titled *Fat, Sick, and Nearly Dead*.

Then she did something smart (and unusual). She emailed friends and family to announce that she was embarking on a sixty-day juicing program—and asked for their help.

That's how I was introduced to Emily R. One of her email recipients was her uncle Mark, who is my longtime literary agent and writing partner. He's also well versed in the Daily Questions process. He offered to coach Emily as she took on a behavioral challenge.

Emily's story is an instructive template not only in the mechanics of doing Daily Questions right—picking the questions, keeping score, monitoring yourself, sticking with it—but in the choices and tweaks we make that influence the outcome.

When I meet clients, I'm casually forming a "change profile" in my head to gauge how much the clients can take on—

and what they should leave for another time. I consider their commitment, their track record of success, and how much social interaction and self-control their change requires. Emily presented with four factors, not all of them working to her advantage:

✔**She asked for help.**
This is good. When we advertise our desire to change, we are openly risking failure, putting our reputation and self-respect on the line. It's the difference between betting on ourselves with hard-earned cash and settling for a friendly no-money wager.

✔**She was going solo.**
Losing weight targets solo rather than interpersonal behavior. When we decide, for example, to be a better listener, our success requires the participation of other people. We have to display our new behavior consistently so that people recognize we're listening more than we're talking. We can't claim we're a better listener; others must claim it for us. Emily was in a different situation. She'd be losing weight on her own, grading herself, not being graded by others. If she faltered, she'd only disappoint herself. She was working in isolation, which meant she had total control over her destiny. All things considered, going solo had to work to her advantage.

✔**She was in a "hostile" environment.**
Emily wasn't doing herself any favors working at Whole Foods. Not only was she spending her workdays in a food emporium of abundance and temptation, but she was also put in charge of the cheese department. Like an alcoholic working

at a brewery, she wasn't in the most conducive environment for promoting weight loss.

✔She had no track record of success.
Emily presented a success profile I'm not accustomed to. Unlike my business clients, she didn't have a lengthy track record of achievement and overcoming challenges. She was young, just starting her professional life, and, in fact, had already failed several times at weight loss.

That's a significant disadvantage compared to successful businesspeople. To them, taking on challenges and succeeding is like exercising a muscle. The more you use it, the stronger it gets—which instills confidence that success will happen in *any* situation.

When I first worked with Alan Mulally in 2001, he was running the commercial aviation division of Boeing. He patiently listened as I outlined my approach. "I get it," he said. "This is a replicable process."

"Well, there's more to it than that," I started to say.

Alan chuckled. "I've built the Boeing 777. I think I can do this."

He was right. Successful people show up with an arsenal of previous achievements that they can apply to new challenges. Alan was my fastest learning assignment ever because he already knew what to do.* Emily didn't have that backstop of achievement. She would not only be developing new eating

---

*The truism that "success breeds success" is the main reason I can commit two years to coaching very successful people with no guarantee until it's all over that I'll get paid. With successful people, the odds are decidedly in my favor.

habits, new behavior. She'd be learning *how to succeed* on the fly.

This was the "change profile" Emily brought to the party on day one. She was tackling one of the hardest behavioral changes in a nonconducive work environment and doing it alone rather than in a supportive group environment.

On the other hand, the Daily Questions and her uncle's nightly follow-up calls would be providing elements of structure and follow-up that are curiously missing from most diet books and weight loss programs (the ones that tell you *what* to eat but not *how* to stick with it). The process she followed is a primer on how to pursue adult behavioral change.

Her first step was deciding what to change. Emily settled on six goals:

- Stick to the juice cleanse.
- Get exercise daily.
- Advance my wine knowledge (she was studying for her Stage 2 Master Sommelier exam).
- Stay in touch with friends and family.
- Learn something new at work.
- Do something nice for someone outside of work.

Her goals, not surprisingly, could have been plucked from the classic self-improvement menu we all feast on: lose weight, get fit, get organized, learn something new, quit a bad habit, save more money, help others, spend more time with family, travel to new places, fall in love, and be less stressed. Nothing wrong with that. The fact that other people have similar goals doesn't make those goals less worthy.

Her next step was embracing the concept of active questions to focus on *effort* rather than *results*. She would phrase her goals as "Did I do my best to . . ." rather than "Did I . . ." Every night at ten o'clock her uncle would call and she would have her scores ready. Thus, the process of change commenced. With her Daily Questions and nightly follow-up by her uncle Mark, there was no turning back. Here are her scores for Weeks 1 thru 4:

EMILY'S DAILY QUESTIONS Did I do my best to:	Days in **weeks 1 & 2**													
	1	2	3	4	5	6	7	8	9	10	11	12	13	14
Stick to the juice cleanse?	10	10	10	10	10	10	10	10	10	10	10	10	10	10
Exercise today?	0	0	0	0	0	0	0	2	0	0	0	0	9	9
Advance my wine knowledge?	2	3	0	0	0	1	4	10	10	8	7	6	9	9
Stay in touch with friends and family?	8	5	6	4	6	3	3	5	5	3	8	4	8	4
Learn something new at work?	3	2	2	6	7	10	0	4	9	3	3	10	9	0
Do something nice for someone outside work?	5	10	10	4	4	6	5	6	3	3	7	7	3	10
Total	28	30	28	24	27	30	22	37	37	27	35	37	48	42

Did I do my best to:	Days in **weeks 3 & 4**													
	15	16	17	18	19	20	21	22	23	24	25	26	27	28
Stick to the juice cleanse?	10	10	10	10	10	10	10	10	10	10	10	10	9	10
Exercise today?	8	0	8	8	10	8	8	9	9	10	10	9	10	10
Advance my wine knowledge?	8	8	7	8	8	8	8	10	10	8	8	10	8	9
Stay in touch with friends and family?	4	5	3	3	6	4	5	3	4	5	7	7	3	2
Learn something new at work?	4	4	10	5	0	4	4	7	8	2	2	8	0	0
Do something nice for someone outside work?	6	10	7	6	7	7	8	4	3	3	5	5	5	8
Total	40	37	45	40	41	41	43	42	44	38	42	49	35	39

One of the unappreciated benefits of Daily Questions is that they force us to quantify an unfamiliar data point: *our level of trying.* We rarely do that. We treat effort as a second-class citizen. It's the condolence message we send ourselves when we fail. We say, "I gave it my best shot," or "I get an A for effort." But after a few days, quantifying effort rather than outcome reveals patterns that we'd otherwise miss.

For example, in Emily's first twelve days, she awarded herself perfect 10s on following her juicing program. That kind of discipline at the start of any change process is not surprising given our natural enthusiasm in the early stages of anything. The shorter the time gap between our planning and our doing, the greater the chance that we'll remember our plan. As the time between planning and doing increases—and our environment intrudes with all its temptations and distractions—our enthusiasm and discipline fade.

But on her next-priority goal, getting some daily exercise, she scored eleven zeros and a single 2 (she went for a walk that day). Her uncle pointed out that a goal can't be that important if you ignore it for nearly two weeks. Why have it on your list at all?

That was a wake-up call for Emily—a bit of "tough love," she called it—forcing her to acknowledge that an extreme weight loss regimen was unhealthy unless accompanied by exercise. The next day she joined a local YMCA with a pool and blocked out an hour for swimming laps. You can see the precise moment on the spreadsheet at Day 13 when she awards herself a 9 on "Did I do my best to exercise today?" By Day 24 she adds a beginners class at Bikram Yoga to her fitness routine. She nearly faints during the ninety-minute class in a room heated to 92 degrees—and scores her first 10. At the end of four weeks, she's 35 pounds lighter.

The next four weeks are more of the same, with some ups and downs and some insights about what matters, what works, what can be left behind. Here are her scores:

EMILY'S DAILY QUESTIONS					Days in **weeks 5 & 6**								
Did I do my best to:	**29**	**30**	**31**	**32**	**33**	**34**	**35**	**36**	**37**	**38**	**39**	**40**	**41**	**42**
Stick to the juice cleanse?	10	10	10	10	10	10	10	10	10	10	10	2	2	2
Exercise today?	8	8	10	9	10	3	3	10	10	10	10	8	8	8
Advance my wine knowledge?	7	8	9	9	10	9	10	10	10	10	10	5	5	5
Stay in touch with friends and family?	9	8	8	6	4	5	6	9	0	3	1	10	10	10
Learn something new at work?	4	5	4	3	7	4	3	0	1	4	7	0	0	0
Do something nice for someone outside work?	6	5	5	5	3	2	6	7	6	5	8	4	4	2
Total	44	44	46	42	44	33	38	46	37	42	46	29	29	27

					Days in **weeks 7 & 8**								
Did I do my best to:	**43**	**44**	**45**	**46**	**47**	**48**	**49**	**50**	**51**	**52**	**53**	**54**	**55**	**56**
Stick to the juice cleanse?	10	10	10	10	10	10	10	10	10	10	10	10	10	10
Exercise today?	8	8	8	10	8	6	10	9	10	10	8	4	10	10
Advance my wine knowledge?	7	8	8	10	7	10	10	10	9	10	2	6	10	10
Stay in touch with friends and family?	9	5	4	7	5	7	6	3	-	-	-	-	-	-
Learn something new at work?	4	4	4	6	3	6	6	-	-	-	-	-	-	-
Do something nice for someone outside work?	6	9	9	3	6	3	3	5	-	-	-	-	-	-
Total	44	44	43	46	39	42	45	43	29	30	20	20	30	30

The line of consecutive 10s on juicing is impressive. It means total effort for Emily, which translates into total compliance—no faltering, no deviating, no cheating with any food that can't be poured out of a bottle. There's a blip at Days 40–42 when her juicing scores drop precipitously. But it's by design. She attends a friend's wedding in Maine and decides to take a break, to not be "that girl" drinking from a juice bottle while everyone else is toasting the couple with champagne and cake. The physical shock of solid food is so discomfiting she welcomes resuming the juice cleanse—and extends the sixty-day program by three days to make up for her "hiatus."

We can also see a sharp uptick on Question 3 about

advancing her wine knowledge. Her sommelier test in New York City is fast approaching (Day 49) and she's cramming, giving herself 9s and 10s for devoting all her free time to study.

At Day 51, we can see the start of a string of blank spaces for Questions 4–6. Emily has concluded that she doesn't need to measure these objectives anymore. They come naturally to her and therefore are not actions at which she has to challenge herself to "do my best." She's winnowed her goals down to three items. That's more than enough. She's not giving up; she's letting go (a valuable skill we'll return to in Chapter 13).

EMILY'S DAILY QUESTIONS			Days in **week 9**				
Did I do my best to:	**57**	**58**	**59**	**60**	**61**	**62**	**63**
Stick to the juice cleanse?	10	10	10	10	10	10	10
Exercise today?	8	8	10	10	9	10	10
Advance my wine knowledge?	7	6	4	9	9	7	9
Stay in touch with friends and family?	-	-	-	-	-	-	-
Learn something new at work?	-	-	-	-	-	-	-
Do something nice for someone outside work?	-	-	-	-	-	-	-
Total	**25**	**24**	**24**	**29**	**28**	**27**	**29**

On Day 63, when she stopped the strict juicing program, Emily had lost 56 pounds. She had also passed her Stage 2 Master Sommelier exam. She was swimming or going to yoga classes at least five days a week. She had achieved the longest sustained stretch of planned behavioral change in her young life. She was feeling good about herself.

The hard part was just beginning.

As discussed in Chapter 8, we change by creating, preserving, accepting, or eliminating. So far Emily was focused on eliminating. After years of bad eating habits, she opted for extreme denial, sacrificing solid food in order to shock her system, reset her metabolism, and jump-start rapid weight loss.

But man or woman does not live by juice alone. After two months Emily knew she would have to stop her program of severe deprivation. The juice cleanse had done its job. It gave her a rigid structure and severely narrowed the eating choices she had to make each day. When your dining options are between a tall glass of kale, celery, and mango juice and a tall glass of liquid sweet potato, carrot, red peppers, red beets, and apple, it's well-nigh impossible to make a decision you'll regret. You can't be tempted by a plate of cheese and crackers, or a bowl of ice cream, or even a healthy handful of almonds if you banish them from your environment.

Now Emily would have to come up with cooking and eating habits that went beyond the quick fix of juicing. She was entering a second phase of behavioral change, one where she was *creating* rather than eliminating. The old Daily Questions no longer applied. She needed to retool her goals into a plan that made sense for the rest of her life. Here's what she came up with:

EMILY'S DAILY QUESTIONS: PHASE 2	Days in **weeks 10 & 11**									
Did I do my best to:	64	65	66	67	68	69	70	71	72	73
Challenge myself physically?	-	-	-	-	-	-	-	-	-	
Eat clean for my body?	-	-	-	-	-	-				
Advance my wine knowledge?	-	-	-	-	-	-	-			
Challenge myself mentally?	-	-	-	-	-	-	-	-	-	
Total	-	-	-	-	-	-	-			

And so it went for nearly a year during which Emily lost an additional 55 pounds and hit her target weight. She also passed her Stage 3 Master Sommelier exam (only the final and absurdly difficult Stage 4 exam remains). And ran her first 5K race.

All in all, a story with a happy ending—although "ending" is a misnomer. Emily's story is ongoing, with no firm expiration date. Like each of us, she is always at risk of reverting to previous undesirable behavior. Tales of backsliding after extreme weight loss are clichés (two-thirds of people regain all the lost weight after three years). Our environment— that mocking rascal waging war against our best interests— makes that a certainty. We must always be vigilant. We can always get better at something, even if it's just preserving the progress we've made.

I cite Emily's story because her primary goal—weight management—is something all but a handful of genetically blessed people can relate to. It's not complicated by the responses of other people, so we can measure it easily. Also, weight loss is custom-made for self-monitoring, because we shape our day around meals. We buy and prepare our food or tell other people what we want. We control our environment; it doesn't control us.

Those are huge advantages not present in most attempts at behavioral change, whether it's a heavy goal like managing our anger or a lighter one like eliminating the F-bomb from our vocabulary. This is where Daily Questions can be a game-changer. They create a more congenial environment for us to succeed at behavioral change, in several ways:

1. They reinforce our commitment.

Daily Questions are what behavioral economists refer to as a "commitment device." The questions announce our intention to do something and, at the risk of private disappointment or public humiliation, they commit us to doing it. Emily asking for help from friends and family is a commitment device. So is setting an alarm clock at night, which commits us to waking up on time. I know people who brush their teeth early in the evening as a commitment device to avoid late-night snacking, in the dubious hope that they'd rather stifle a food craving than re-brush before bedtime. A "swear jar" to which we donate cash every time we use vulgar language is a common commitment device. So is betting with friends that we'll finish a project on time, the loss of money presumably spurring us on to success (right!). So are social media sites that ask us to sign a "contract" to change our behavior and use our credit card to penalize us financially (for example, donating to a favorite charity, or more chilling, to a cause we loathe) when we falter. So are software programs like Freedom that let people shut down Internet access for eight hours and apps like Lose It! that put a ceiling on daily caloric intake based on how quickly we want to lose weight. Our commitment devices are as clever and goofy and numerous as the mental gyrations we employ to do something. Even for-profit corporations have gotten into the act. The eyeglass maker Warby Parker reorganized itself as a "B corporation," formally committing to social progress as much as profit, so that its business model means distributing a free pair of glasses in the developing world for every pair it sells. It can't abandon the mission on a whim or when business slows down without facing legal and reputational damage. That's a serious commitment device.

Daily Questions are serious, too, if only in how they press us to articulate what we really want to change in our lives. For many of us, listing our goals may be the first time we've acknowledged our faults or considered changing or committed to getting better. (Can you remember the moment when you initiated your first significant adult behavioral change? What triggered it? How well did you do? A better question: Have you ever actually changed your behavior as an adult?)

2. They ignite our motivation where we need it, not where we don't.

Generally speaking, we are guided by two kinds of motivation.

Intrinsic motivation is wanting to do something for its own sake, because we enjoy it; for example, reading a book that *isn't* assigned in class, simply because we're curious about the subject. People who get up early to run six miles for the pure pleasure of physical exertion are high in intrinsic motivation for that particular activity. So are the devoted home cooks who'll spend hours baking a perfect loaf of bread that they could easily buy at a bakery. Likewise, people who spend their Sunday mornings doing the crossword puzzle. Pleasure, devotion, curiosity are telltale signs of intrinsic motivation.

Extrinsic motivation is doing something for external rewards such as other people's approval or to avoid punishment. We are bombarded with extrinsic motivators during our school years—grades, awards, scholarships, parental pressure, resumé building, acceptance into prestige schools. These external drivers don't vanish when we enter the workforce. They just assume different names: salary, job title, office size, recognition, fame, expense account, Black Card, vacation home, etc.—all the trophies that inspire us to work hard and behave well. Our extrinsic motivation gets shaky only when we achieve these targets—and wonder why they haven't provided the meaning, purpose, and happiness we were hoping for.

Daily Questions focus us on where we need help, not where we're doing just fine. We all have tasks and behaviors that come naturally to us, where we don't need a boost from an outside agency. For example, speaking in front of audiences is the most enjoyable thing I do. It's a major source of income. It drives sales of books like the one you're reading. It's where I expend the greatest effort as a professional—whether I'm getting paid or working pro bono, whether it's a thirty-minute speech to six people or four ninety-minute sessions in a row to hundreds of people. And yet my public speaking would never come up as a Daily Question—because I don't need to monitor my motivation as a speaker. In this area, I'm already maxed out. I love doing it and hope to continue as long as I can.

Of course, there are many areas where our motivation—intrinsic or extrinsic—is less than optimal. Daily Questions press us to face them, admit them, and write them down. Until we can do that, we have no chance of getting better.

3. They highlight the difference between self-discipline and self-control.

Behavioral change demands self-discipline and self-control. We tend to use these terms interchangeably, but there's a subtle difference. Self-discipline refers to *achieving desirable behavior.* Self-control refers to *avoiding undesirable behavior.*

When we wake up in the dark morning hours to hit the gym, or run a weekly meeting so that it ends on time, or leave work with a clean desk, or remember to thank our colleagues for helping us, we're displaying self-discipline—repeating positive actions consistently. When we deny ourselves that which we most enjoy—whether it's stifling the urge to crack wise at someone else's expense or saying no to a second helping of dessert—we're displaying self-control.

Most people are better at one than the other. They're good at repeating positive actions, not so good at avoiding negative ones. Or vice versa. This disconnect explains the walking oxymorons among us—the strict vegetarians who smoke, the flabby personal trainers, the accountants declaring personal bankruptcy, the executive coaches who need their own coach.

We reveal our preference for self-discipline or self-control in the way we phrase our Daily Questions. It's one thing to ask ourselves, "Did I do my best to limit my sugar consumption?" and another to ask, "Did I do my best to say no to sweets?" The former calls for self-discipline, the latter self-control. Depending on who we are, that subtle adjustment can make all the difference.

4. They shrink our goals into manageable increments.

More than anything, Daily Questions neutralize the arch-enemy of behavioral change: our *impatience.* Whether it's flat abs or a new reputation, we want to see results now, not later. We see the gap between the effort required today and the reward we'll reap in an undetermined future—and lose our enthusiasm for change. We crave instant gratification and chafe at the prospect of prolonged trying.

Daily Questions, by definition, compel us to take things one day at a time. In doing so they shrink our objectives into manageable twenty-four-hour increments.

By focusing on effort, they distract us from our obsession with results (because that's not what we're measuring). In turn, we are free to appreciate the process of change and our role in making it happen. We're no longer frustrated by the languid pace of visible progress—because we're looking in another direction.

Daily Questions remind us that:

- Change doesn't happen overnight.
- Success is the sum of small efforts repeated day in and day out.
- If we make the effort, we will get better. If we don't, we won't.

Commitment. Motivation. Self-discipline. Self-control. Patience. Those are powerful allies when we try to change our ways, courtesy of Daily Questions.

There's one other ally we've left out of this discussion—the coach.

Chapter 12

Planner, Doer, *and* Coach

There's no inherent magic to charting our Daily Questions on a spreadsheet. A spreadsheet is clean and organized and readily shows if we're trending in the right direction. But the spreadsheet is not essential. Nor is the nightly phone call for reporting scores. The format of communication is not the difference maker.

The only essential element is that the scores are reported somehow—via direct phone contact, email, or a voice message—to someone every day. And that someone is the coach.

For some people the "coach" is little more than a scorekeeper—someone we report to each evening without having to endure any judgment or interference. For others the coach is a referee, someone keeping score but also blowing the whistle when we commit an egregious foul (for example, pressing us to explain several days of low scores). For others the coach is a full-blown adviser, engaging us in a dialogue about what we're doing and why.

At the most basic level, a coach is a follow-up mechanism, like a supervisor who regularly checks in on how we're doing (we're more productive when we know we're being watched from above).

At a slightly more sophisticated level, a coach instills accountability. In the self-scoring system of Daily Questions, we must answer for our answers. If we're displeased, we face a choice. Do we continue suffering our self-created disappointment, or do we try harder? As a result, reading off our scores every night to a "coach" becomes a daily test of our commitment—a good thing given our inclination to bear down when we know we'll be tested.

But a "coach" is more than a surrogate for our guilty conscience.

At the highest level, a coach is a source of mediation, bridging the gap between the visionary Planner and short-sighted Doer in us. The Planner in us may say "I'm going to read *Anna Karenina* over vacation," but during a holiday packed with enticing distractions, it's the Doer who has to find a quiet corner and get through Tolstoy's many pages. A Coach reminds us of the unreliable person we become after we make our plans. A Coach reminds the fragile Doer what he's supposed to do. It's a simple dynamic that looks like this:

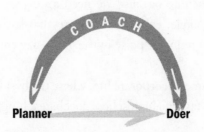

Most of us are already familiar with this dynamic. If we want to get in shape, we sign up with a trainer (a common form of "coach"). We make an appointment for 10:30 a.m. on a Tuesday, with the full intention of working out with the trainer. Come Tuesday morning we're not so sure. A friend needs a ride to the airport. We stayed out late the night before. We stubbed our toe. The shoelace broke on our cross trainers. The excuses are endless, some legitimate, most lame. The eager Planner in us has become a reluctant Doer.

But the trainer's presence in this dynamic changes everything. We have to show up because the trainer's expecting us. Maybe she's driving a long way to meet us. Maybe she's passed up other appointments to fit us in. As a human being we have an obligation to her. There's also a monetary issue: we're paying her whether or not we show up. Plus, there's the mild humiliation of canceling the first appointment; we're failing before we even begin.

All of these factors—shame, guilt, cost, obligation, decency—conspire to influence us, solely because of the trainer's presence. This is how we do what we intend to do. The Coach meshes our inner Planner with our inner Doer. This is how successful change happens: in situations big or small, we make choices that marry intention with execution.

We know this intuitively in most endeavors. In sports, we welcome coaching because we need an expert eye correcting our technique, exhorting us to try harder, and reminding us to maintain our poise in the game-day environment of competition.

It's the same in corporate life, where the best leaders function like our favorite high school coach: teaching, supporting,

inspiring us, and occasionally instilling some healthy para-
noia to keep us surging ahead.

But beyond the structured hierarchies of the workplace,
where we're always answerable to someone for our paycheck
and where we have clear incentives for getting better, we don't
appreciate the dynamic as well. In our private lives, where our
chaotic environment triggers undesirable behavior, we don't
always welcome coaching.

One reason we resist coaching, I'm sure, is our need for
privacy. Some pieces of us are not to be shared with the world.
It's one thing to admit we could shed some pounds or be in
better shape; it's practically a badge of honor, a testament to
our candor and self-improvement ambitions. It's another thing
to confess that we're lacking as a partner or parent—that is, as
a decent "person"—and own up to that personal failing every
day. We prefer to keep some of our behavioral deficits to ourselves rather than hang them out in public like laundry.

Another reason is that we don't know that we need to
change. We are in denial, convincing ourselves that others
need help, not us. In 2005 the CEO of a large West Coast
equipment company called me in to work with his COO and
heir apparent. The CEO had a precise timetable for succes-
sion. "My number two is a good guy," he said, "but he needs
three more years of seasoning. Then I'll be ready to leave, he
can take over, and everything's good." My antennae perk up
whenever I'm asked to conduct research that proves someone's predetermined conclusion. Something wasn't right. Sure
enough, when I finished my 360-degree interviews with the
COO's colleagues, they all said the number two was "ready
now." The deeper problem was the CEO. Without prompting,

nearly every interviewee said the CEO had stayed too long and should leave for the good of the company.

Then there's the successful person's unshakable self-sufficiency: we think we can do it all on our own. Quite often we can, of course. But what's the virtue of saying no to help? It's a needless vanity, a failure to recognize change's degree of difficulty. I know this because behavioral change—talking about it, writing books about it, helping others achieve it—is my life. And yet I have to pay a woman named Kate to call me every night to follow up on how I'm doing! This isn't professional hypocrisy, as if I'm a chef who won't eat his own cooking. It's a public admission that I'm weak. We're all weak. The process of change is hard enough without grabbing all the help we can get.

The irony is that, although the process of Daily Questions and coaching works just fine with the get-thin, get-fit, get-organized goals of our New Year's resolutions, it's even better, practically custom-made, for interpersonal challenges—the be-nice, be-appreciative, be-caring, be-awake goals that make other people feel better, not worse, for knowing us. I know this because it's what I work on with my clients. They don't ask me to help them become better strategists, budgeters, negotiators, public speakers, proposal writers, or programmers. I help them become better role models in their relationships with the people who matter most to them—their family, their friends, their colleagues, their customers.

Not long ago I worked with an executive named Griffin whose behavioral issue was adding too much value at work.*

---

*Readers of my 2007 book, *What Got You Here Won't Get You There*, may recall this issue from my list of twenty workplace habits we all need to break, along with "Winning too much" and "Speaking when

If one of his people came in with a new idea, instead of saying "Great idea," he displayed an uncontrollable urge to improve it. Sometimes his contribution was helpful, other times questionable. The problem was, while he may have improved the content of the idea by 10 percent, he reduced the employee's ownership of the idea by 50 percent. He was stifling debate and creativity—and driving away talent. He was a quick study and with Daily Questions was soon awarding himself 10s for *not* adding value. It took nearly a year for his staff to catch up and fully accept the change and not get jumpy when presenting him with new ideas. But he got better and I got paid.

It was such a quick and painless process—we became friends—that I volunteered to coach Griffin on something else. (Like most people, I get enthusiastic about stuff that works.)

"Pick an issue at home," I said. "Let's see if you can improve on that."

He was a little embarrassed with his pick. He called it the Clinking Cubes Problem.

There were certain sounds, all associated with beverages, that annoyed him: the glug-glug sound of someone gulping down a bottle of water; the exaggerated hissing of soda being poured over a glass of ice; and the clinking of ice cubes in a mixed drink. Other sounds didn't faze him—not barking dogs or howling babies or fingernails on a blackboard. "Not even Josh Groban's singing," he said.

"How's this a problem?" I asked. "Cover your ears. Leave the room."

---

angry" and "Punishing the messenger" and "Telling the world how smart we are."

It had only become a problem recently when his wife switched from mineral water out of a bottle to diet cola over ice. She'd swirl the ice cubes in her glass, take a sip, swirl some more—and the sound would send Griffin up the wall. The point of having a drink with his wife was to create a relaxing environment and reconnect once a day. But suddenly their evening ritual was as stressful as visiting the dentist for a root canal.

One evening Griffin couldn't take it anymore. He yelled at her, "Will you stop clinking!"

His wife stared at him and said, "Really?" But the look on her face meant, *You're an idiot.*

Griffin knew she was right. She wasn't doing anything wrong. He was out of line if he expected her, not him, to change. Admitting the problem was a good first step.

The second step was seeing the relaxing evening hour as a hostile environment of his own creation—and adding a new item to his list of Daily Questions. *Did I do my best to enjoy the hour with my wife?* If he created the problem, he could solve it.

On a scale of 1 to 10, his goal was to score a 10 for effort every day. He would try to contain his discomfort, ignore the sound, pretend he was enjoying himself—all in the name of not upsetting his wife. It was an exercise in being a good husband, which was important to Griffin.

The first days of enduring the clinking, he told me, "I almost shattered my glass from gripping it so hard. But I didn't complain. I didn't make my distress visible."

At night, when he emailed me his score, he gave himself top marks for trying so hard. After a couple of weeks of adhering to this strategy, his irritation began to diminish. Not completely but gradually, as if someone were turning down the volume knob one click every day. Within a month the problem was gone, like he'd cured a bad habit. He'd conditioned his mind to respond differently. The clinking cubes triggered indifference—a lukewarm "Meh!"—instead of annoyance and anger. Griffin couldn't change his environment, so he changed how he reacted to it.

Admittedly, Griffin was one of my prize coaching clients. Like a physically gifted athlete who can instantly adopt a coach's instruction and turn bad technique into good, he believed in Daily Questions *and* checked himself daily. He was good at the process—and changed. I mention this episode because it highlights three benefits of Daily Questions:

1. If we do it, we get better.

This is one of the minor miracles of Daily Questions. If we do them consistently and properly (and let's face it, how much skill do we need to score ourselves on effort?), we get better. We don't get many guarantees in life, but this is one of them. My clients get better if they listen to me. They don't if they do nothing.

2. We get better faster.

Griffin only needed a month to solve his Clinking Cubes Problem—as if after eighteen months of being coached at work, he not only got better, but he became more efficient at the process of getting better.

We expect this sort of progress with activities that require physical dexterity, from cooking an omelet to performing heart surgery. The more we correctly repeat an action the more adept we become at executing it—like a dancer who after years of training her muscle memory can repeat a complex series of steps in one try rather than two or three.

We don't expect this progress as readily with our warm and fuzzy emotional goals. They're not technique driven. They're influenced by other people's responses and a changing environment. But it happens. I see this with many of my one-on-one clients *after* we part ways. Like Griffin, once they've learned how to change one behavior, they can do it again with another behavior—more smoothly and swiftly than the first time.

3. Eventually we become our own Coach.

This is the most astonishing benefit: eventually we become the Coach. I know this is true because of all my clients who got better—and continued improving without me.

It makes sense given the gap between the Farsighted Planner and Myopic Doer in us. Coaches can bridge that gap because they're objective, not caught up in the environment that so often corrupts us. They can remind us of our original intentions. They can recall the times when we displayed desirable behavior and help us summon up the will to do so again. That's what Coaches do. But over time, after many reminders, we learn and adapt. We recognize the situations where we'll likely stray from our plans. We think, "I've been here before. I know what works and what doesn't." And after many failures, one day we make a better choice. (This should not surprise us. It would be surprising if we *didn't* learn, if we *didn't* behave correctly after making the same mistake for the hundredth time in a familiar situation.)

That's the moment when the Planner and Doer in us are joined by the Coach in us. We don't need an outside agency to point out our behavioral danger zones, or urge us to toe the line, or even hear our nightly scores. We can do it on our own.

The Coach in us takes many forms. It can be an inner voice, akin to conscience, whispering in our ear to remember an earlier time when we did the right thing. It can be a song lyric, a spiritual talisman, a meaningful motto, an instruction on a card, a memory of someone important to us, anything that triggers desired behavior.

It can even be a photograph. This one coaches me:

It is the only framed photo in my study at home. It was taken by an Associated Press photographer in Mali, Africa, in 1984. I was getting started in my coaching practice and working as a volunteer with Richard Schubert, CEO of the American Red Cross.

Sub-Saharan Africa was experiencing a massive drought.

Hundreds of thousands of people were facing starvation. Richard asked me to join eight other Americans on a fact-finding mission to Mali. Our trip was featured for a week on NBC News.

The picture shows the thirty-five-year-old me kneeling next to a Red Cross professional in the Sahara Desert. Behind her is a line of children between the ages of two and sixteen.

The food supply in Mali was extremely limited, so the Red Cross was introducing triage. Any available food would be handed out to children between the ages of two and sixteen on the chilling assumption that children under two would almost certainly die and those over sixteen might survive on their own.

The woman from the Red Cross was measuring children's arms to determine who ate, who didn't. If their arms were too large, they were "not hungry enough" and given no food. If their arms were too small, they were beyond saving and also given no food. If their arms were in the midrange, they were given a small portion of the available food.

I'd need a sociopath's personality to be unmoved by the experience. But as I returned home to my "normal" life, there was a good chance the memory, no matter how searing, would gradually recede in power. Except I have this photo.

The picture triggers gratitude, as if the 1984 me is coaching today's me. It sends a simple message:

Be grateful for what you have. No matter the disappointment or supposed tribulation, do not whine or complain, do not get angry, do not lash out at another person to express your entitlement. You are no better than these African children. Their terrible fate, undeserved and tragic, could have been your fate. Never forget this day.

And I never do. The photo comes to my mind almost daily because life is glutted with "supposed tribulations." For example, have you ever observed how people in airports react to the announcement that their plane is delayed? It's one of life's more reliable negative triggers. People get agitated. They fume and sulk and lose their composure, often in front of innocent airline employees. I used to be one of those people, not a raging public spectacle perhaps, but certainly someone who felt victimized. I didn't like the feeling, because after the starving children of Mali, I knew I hadn't earned the right to victimhood. I associate that unmerited feeling with the photo. For years now, when I hear that my plane will be delayed I remember the photo and repeat this mantra: "Never complain because the airplane is late. There are people in the world who have problems you cannot imagine. You are a lucky man." The photo is a positive trigger in an otherwise negative environment.

Chapter 13

AIWATT

Every endeavor comes with a first principle that dramatically improves our chances of success at that endeavor.

- In carpentry it's *Measure twice, cut once.*
- In sailing it's *Know where the wind is coming from.*
- In women's fashion it's *Buy a little black dress.*

I have a first principle for becoming the person you want to be. Follow it and it will shrink your daily volume of stress, conflict, unpleasant debate, and wasted time. It is phrased in the form of a question you should be asking yourself whenever you must choose to either engage or "let it go."

Am I willing,
at this time,
to make the investment required
to make a positive difference
on this topic?

It's a question that pops into my head so often each day that I've turned the first five words into an acronym, AIWATT (it rhymes with "say what"). Like the physician's principle, *First, do no harm*, it doesn't require you to do anything, merely avoid doing something foolish.

The question is a mash-up of two bits of guidance I've valued over the years, one part Buddhist insight, the other part common sense from the late Peter Drucker.

It's Always an Empty Boat

The Buddhist wisdom is contained in the Parable of the Empty Boat:

> A young farmer was covered with sweat as he paddled his boat up the river. He was going upstream to deliver his produce to the village. It was a hot day, and he wanted to make his delivery and get home before dark. As he looked ahead, he spied another vessel, heading rapidly downstream toward his boat. He rowed furiously to get out of the way, but it didn't seem to help.
>
> He shouted, "Change direction! You are going to hit me!" To no avail. The vessel hit his boat with a violent thud. He cried out, "You idiot! How could you manage to hit my boat in the middle of this wide river?" As he glared into the boat, seeking out the individual responsible for the accident, he realized no one was there. He had been screaming at an empty boat that had broken free of its moorings and was floating downstream with the current.

We behave one way when we believe that there is another person at the helm. We can blame that stupid, uncaring person for our misfortune. This blaming permits us to get angry, act out, assign blame, and play the victim.

We behave more calmly when we learn that it's an empty boat. With no available scapegoat, we can't get upset. We make peace with the fact that our misfortune was the result of fate or bad luck. We may even laugh at the absurdity of a random unmanned boat finding a way to collide with us in a vast body of water.

The moral: there's never anyone in the other boat. We are always screaming at an empty vessel. An empty boat isn't targeting us. And neither are all the people creating the sour notes in the soundtrack of our day.

- The colleague who always interrupts you in meetings? He thinks he's smarter than everyone, not just you. Empty boat.
- The aggressive driver who tailgated you for miles on the way to work today? He does that every day on any road. That's how he rolls. Empty car.
- The bank officer who turned down your small business loan application because of a typo on the form? He sees a form, not you. Empty suit.
- The checkout woman at the supermarket who neglected to pack the small tin of gourmet anchovies you need for tonight's dinner party, so you have to drive back to the market to pick up what you paid for? She's been scanning and packing items all day. A three-ounce tin is easy to miss. She didn't do it

intentionally, certainly not to you. Another empty vessel.

I like to make this point in leadership classes with a simple exercise. I'll ask a random audience member to think of one person who makes him or her feel bad, angry, or crazy. "Can you envision that person?" I ask.

A nod, a disgusted face, and then, "Yes."

"How much sleep is that person losing over you tonight?" I ask.

"None."

"Who is being punished here? Who is doing the punishing?" I ask.

The answer inevitably is "Me and me."

I end the exercise with a simple reminder that getting mad at people for being who they are makes as much sense as getting mad at a chair for being a chair. The chair cannot help but be a chair, and neither can most of the people we encounter. If there's a person who drives you crazy, you don't have to like, agree with, or respect him, just accept him for being who he is.

Don Corleone, the Godfather, must have been a closet Buddhist when he said, "It's not personal. It's business." He knew that people disappoint us or disagree with us when it's in their best interest to do so, not because they want to cause us pain. It's the same with all the people who annoy or enrage us. They're doing it because that's who they are, not because of who we are.

Creating False Positives

The common sense comes from Peter Drucker, who said, "Our mission in life should be to make a positive difference, not to prove how smart or right we are." The advice sounds anodyne and obvious. Given the choice, who wouldn't opt to make a "positive difference"?

But Drucker is highlighting two notions that we have trouble holding in our heads simultaneously. When we have the opportunity to demonstrate our brainpower, we're rarely thinking about a positive result for the other people in the room. We're actually issuing what I like to call "false positives"—making statements to upgrade ourselves, often at the expense of others—and they appear in many forms:

- There's *pedantry*. A subordinate makes a grammatical error in a presentation—using *who* instead of *whom*—and you correct him. Smart, perhaps (if the objective is punctilious grammar), but hardly a contribution that improves the room's vibe or how the subordinate feels.
- There's *"I told you so."* You tell your wife the two of you need to leave the house at least sixty minutes in advance to make an eight o'clock Broadway show. She delays, you arrive late, and miss the first scene. You turn petulant, needle her for ruining your night, remind her that you said sixty minutes. You're right, of course—and proceed to ruin her night in proportion to how much she ruined yours.
- There's the *moral superiority* you assert when you tell

a friend or loved one that she shouldn't smoke, that he doesn't need another beer, or that you would have taken a faster route home. How often do these alleged attempts to help elicit a genuine thank-you from the object of your attention?

- There's *complaining* about your managers, your colleagues, your rivals, your customers. (The average American worker spends fifteen hours a month complaining about his or her superiors.) When you complain, you're disagreeing with what someone else decided, planned, or did. By definition, you're being disagreeable—and adding the implication that you would have done better. It's rarely a positive contribution, especially so if you do it behind people's backs rather than to their faces.

This is profoundly counterproductive behavior that achieves the opposite of its intended effect. We don't *instruct* when we correct someone in public for a small error; or *heal* a sore wound with "I told you so"; or *cure* people's bad habits by suggesting they should be more like us; or *improve* our superiors by complaining about them to others.

These are just four random examples of what we do all day. From wake-up to bedtime, when we're in contact with another human being, we face the option of being helpful, hurtful, or neutral. If we're not paying attention we often choose hurtful, largely to prove we're smarter, better, more right than the "other guy."

I've come to regard the "empty boat" parable and Peter Drucker's positivity advice as complementary insights. The Buddhism is inward-facing; it's about maintaining our sanity in the presence of others. The Drucker is outward-facing; it's about confining our contributions to the positive.

When we lash out or belittle others—that is, fail to make a positive contribution to a situation—we're not aware that we're being counterproductive. Nor is it our intention to be cruel, as if we have chosen to speak our minds and "Damn the consequences!" Consequences don't enter the picture. We're only thinking about elevating ourselves. *We're trying to prove how smart we are to an empty boat!*

| | |

AIWATT is the delaying mechanism we should be deploying in the interval between trigger and behavior—after a trigger creates an impulse and before behavior we may regret. AIWATT creates a split-second delay in our prideful, cynical, judgmental, argumentative, and selfish responses to our triggering environment. The delay gives us time to consider a more positive response. The nineteen-word text deserves close parsing:

> *Am I willing* implies that we are exercising volition—taking responsibility—rather than surfing along the waves of inertia that otherwise rule our day. We are asking, "Do I really want to do this?"
>
> *At this time* reminds us that we're operating in the present. Circumstances will differ later on, demanding a different response. The only issue is what we're facing *now.*
>
> *To make the investment required* reminds us that responding to others is work, an expenditure of time, energy, and

opportunity. And, like any investment, our resources are finite. We are asking, "Is this really the best use of my time?"

To make a positive difference places the emphasis on the kinder, gentler side of our nature. It's a reminder that we can help create a better us or a better world. If we're not accomplishing one or the other, why are we getting involved?

On this topic focuses us on the matter at hand. We can't solve every problem. The time we spend on topics where we *can't* make a positive difference is stolen from topics where we *can*.

The circumstances for deploying AIWATT are not limited to those moments when we must choose to be nice or not (although I can't overestimate the importance of being nice). The question matters in the seemingly small moments that can shape our reputation and make or break our relationships. For example:

1. When we confuse disclosure with honesty

We all have the good sense to shade our opinions and tamp down our needless disclosure in the inconsequential moments when doing so costs us nothing. If our mother asks what we think of her new haircut we'll say it looks great, no matter what we think. After all, who wants to crush Mom's feelings over hair? We do this all day long—small omissions that shield the people we love from needless pinpricks of pain.

But that laudable instinct to protect others weakens when it comes up against our need to assert and protect ourselves. In those moments we employ honesty as a weapon rather than as a positive contribution to the situation. Doctors face this dilemma when they must choose between telling a cancer patient the blunt truth (to avoid creating false hope) or sugar-coating the bad news (to uplift the patient, inspire optimism). But at least they debate how much to disclose to the patient. We often don't.

If you've ever broken up badly with a boyfriend or girlfriend and regretted your clumsy, hurtful explanations for parting ways, you can remember the difference between honesty and disclosure. Honesty is stating enough truth to satisfy the other person's need to know. Too much disclosure has a more ambitious reach—often to a point where the other person suffers and feels ashamed.

Likewise in the workplace, when we fire someone, we can use nonjudgmental language like "I'm sorry it didn't work out." Or we can itemize all the ways that the employee is a total dud, crossing the line from honesty to disclosure. It's the interpersonal equivalent of piling on in football or running up the score against a much weaker opponent. We get caught up in the competitive frenzy of the game—the need to win, to assert our superiority—and forget how the other side feels.

Honesty versus disclosure isn't a multilayered conundrum. It's a one-dimensional choice, like taking the Surprise Birthday Party Test. What do you do when a loved one throws a surprise party for you but a friend has let the cat out of the bag? As you enter the room, do you (a) opt for honesty and reveal you already know, (b) opt for disclosure and blame the friend who ruined the surprise, or (c) feign surprise? If you needed time to sift through options (a) and (b) before choosing (c), you've got more work to do in this area.

2. When we have an opinion

In 1960, when A. J. Liebling wrote, "Freedom of the press is guaranteed only to those who own one," he couldn't have foreseen our Age of Social Media, when anyone with a smartphone can behave like an op-ed columnist and "publish" his or her opinion on any subject at any time at any length. It's one of the mixed blessings of twenty-first-century life. It broadens debate and narrows the gap between the powerful and the disenfranchised, but it also wastes a lot of time.

For example, my friend Larry was so proud of a one-star (the lowest rating) Amazon book review he'd posted, he insisted I read it. It was a smart, surgical strike against the author, arguing that the book was a waste of readers' money. It was also very long and meticulously documented with direct quotes and page numbers. Larry must have spent several hours writing it. There were also two dozen comments from readers of the review, which Larry checked several times a day. All in all, he spent a full workday on a book review that might be read by two hundred people.

"Why bother?" I wanted to know.

"Because the author's a fraud and a cheat," he said.

"And you needed the world to know that you were smart enough to spot it?"

"That's part of it," he said.

"What else is there?" I asked.

"I was morally outraged by the book," he said.

"But couldn't you have just let it go and spent those hours more productively?"

"I had to do it and I enjoyed it," he said. "I would have been more upset not doing it."

That was all I needed to hear. Larry had done his private risk-reward analysis and determined that writing a review was worth his time and, in warning readers away from the book, made a positive contribution. He wasn't being a troll. In his mind, he was doing good—and enjoying it.

If only the rest of us were so clearheaded about the reasons we spend so much time voicing unsolicited opinions online—in letters to editors, on personal blogs, on Facebook and Twitter, in product reviews, and so on. I'm not dismissing the value of creating all that crowdsourced information. I'm concerned about all the unquestioned, unregulated time it takes.

Until it becomes obsessive and nasty, online opinionizing is a minor infraction that costs us time, not personal relationships. Most of the time we're "debating" online with strangers, people we do not know and will never meet. It's hardly worth the worry. The bigger problem is when we bring that aggressive voice to work or social occasions and broadcast our opinions to real live people we know—which leads to . . .

3. When our facts collide with other people's beliefs

Confirmation bias—our tendency to favor information that confirms our opinions, whether it's true or not—is an established psychological concept. It afflicts how we gather information (selectively), interpret it (prejudicially), and recall it (unreliably). It comes in many forms—from how we favor sources that confirm our existing attitudes to the way we twist ambiguous or inconvenient facts to support a cherished belief. We're all guilty of this. Parents who see their child's early mastery of toilet training as evidence of genius are displaying confirmation bias. So is a leader who makes a flawed decision after shutting out the room's dissenting voices.

We can't eliminate confirmation bias in others or, for that matter, in ourselves. But we should avoid its more pernicious forms. Of all the pointless debates we can get trapped in, the worst is when facts and beliefs commingle. It never ends well. Whether the subject is climate change or the life span of unicorns, when you cite demonstrable facts to counter another person's belief, a phenomenon that researchers call "the backfire effect" takes over. Your brilliant marshaling of data not only fails to persuade the believer, it backfires and strengthens his or her belief. The believer doubles down on his or her position—and the two of you are more polarized than ever. If you've ever participated in or observed a hot-button debate between an archliberal and archconservative, you know how rare it is for one side to walk away with their opinion altered, or to end up telling their adversary, "You're right. I was wrong. Thank you."

None of this makes sense. At best, you've spent a lot of time failing to change someone's mind. At worst, you've made an enemy, damaged a relationship, and added to your reputation for being disagreeable.

4. When decisions don't go our way

Another Peter Drucker quote changed my life. I tell it to everyone I coach, some would say over and over again: "Every decision in the world is made by the person who has the power to make the decision. Make peace with that."

Again, this sounds obvious, practically a tautology: decision makers make the decisions.

But it's also a reminder about power: decision makers have it, the rest of us don't. Sometimes the decision makers, choices are logical and wise, other times irrational, petty, and foolish. That doesn't change the fact that they are still the decision makers. It's the rare person who can make peace with that fact. From the schoolkid complaining about a teacher's grade to the teen sulking about a parental grounding to the rejected suitor moaning about a lost love to an imperious CEO ignoring his board's directives, we go through life grumbling about *what should be* at the expense of accepting *what is*. Within that bubble of delusion, we grant ourselves an autonomy and superiority we have not earned. We imagine how much better the world would be if we had the power to make the decisions. We don't.

If this is your issue—habitually disagreeing with a decision—AIWATT blesses you with the simplest of cost-benefit analyses: *Is this battle worth fighting?* If your answer is no, put the decision behind you and plant your flag where you can make a positive difference.

If your answer is yes, go for it. For example, I'm contributing a large chunk of my time to helping Dr. Jim Yong Kim of the World Bank in his organization's mission to wipe out extreme poverty. I'm not naïve. I know success won't happen in my lifetime. But I am willing to make the personal investment required to try. There is immeasurable satisfaction—even pleasure—in taking a big risk and fighting a battle you believe in. It's your life, your call. No one else can make it for you. AIWATT prepares you to live with the consequences.

5. When we regret our own decisions

My seatmate on a flight from Europe to the United States was a Switzerland-based private investor. As we exchanged the usual "What do you do?" pleasantries, he told me about a small business he'd acquired and how disappointed he was with the owner whom he had left in charge of the business, which was losing money. He regretted the deal, felt he'd been duped into a bad investment.

"How long has this been going on?" I asked. "This resentment and regret?" (In such moments, I often feel like the Regret Whisperer—which I don't mind.)

"Two years," he said.

"Who are you angry with?" I asked. "The owner for selling, or you for buying?"

He laughed and said, "Good one." No more needed to be said.

When we regret our own decisions—and do nothing about it—we are no better than a whining employee complaining about his superiors. We are yelling at an empty boat, except it's our boat.

AIWATT isn't a universal panacea for all our interpersonal problems. I've given it prominence here because it has a specific utility. It's a reminder that our environment tempts us many times a day to engage in pointless skirmishes. And we can do something about it—by doing nothing.

Like closing our office door so people hesitate before they knock, when we ask ourselves, "Am I willing, at this time, to make the investment required to make a positive difference on this topic?" we have a thin barrier of breathing room, time enough to inhale, exhale, and reflect before we engage or move on. In doing so, we block out the chatter and noise, freeing ourselves to tackle changes that really matter.

Part Three

More Structure, Please

Chapter 14

We Do Not Get Better Without Structure

O f all my coaching clients, the executive who improved the most while spending the least amount of time with me was Alan Mulally. And he was a fantastic leader to start with.

I first met Alan in 2001, when he was president of Boeing Commercial Aircraft, before he became the CEO of Ford Motor Company in 2006. When Alan retired from Ford in 2014, *Fortune* magazine ranked him as the third-greatest leader in the world, behind Pope Francis and Angela Merkel. He and I are now working together to help both nonprofits and major companies develop great leadership teams.

I have learned more from Alan than he has from me—in large part because I've had the opportunity to watch him apply some of the ideas we've discussed on a broad corporate canvas. No idea looms bigger in Alan's mind than the importance of structure in turning around an organization and its people. I believe that the Business Plan Review (BPR) process that he has developed is the most effective use of organizational structure that I have ever observed. In my years of coaching and research on change, I have learned one key lesson, which has near-universal applicability: *We do not get better without structure.*

Alan doesn't merely believe in the value of structure; he lives it and breathes it. When Alan arrived at Ford he instituted weekly Thursday morning meetings, known as the Business Plan Review, or BPR, with his sixteen top executives and the executive's guests from around the world. Not an unusual move (what CEO doesn't have meetings?). But Alan had some rules that were new to Ford veterans. Attendance was mandatory; no exceptions (traveling executives participated by videoconference). No side discussions, no joking at the expense of others, no interruptions, no cell phones, no handing off parts of the presentation to a subordinate. Each leader was expected to articulate his group's plan, status, forecast, and areas that needed special attention. Each leader had a mission to help—not judge—the other people in the room.

So far so good. Every new leader tries to break down the existing culture with new ways of doing old things.

But Alan, who had spent his entire career building jet airplanes, had an aeronautical engineer's faith in structure and process. To get talented people working together, he paid attention to details, all the way down to the granular level. He began each BPR session in the same way: "My name is Alan Mulally and I'm the CEO of Ford Motor Company." Then he'd review the company's plan, status, forecast, and areas that needed special attention, using a green-yellow-red scoring system for good-concerned-poor. He asked his top sixteen executives to do the same, using the same introductory language and color scheme. In effect, he was using the same type of structure that I recommend in my coaching process and applying it to the entire corporation. He was introducing structure to his new team. And he did not deviate, either in content or wording. He always identified himself, always listed his four priorities, always graded his performance for the previous week. He never went off-message, and he expected the executives to follow suit.

At first a few executives thought Alan must be joking. No adult running a giant corporation could possibly believe in this seemingly simple disciplined routine, repeated week after week.

But Alan was serious. Structure was imperative at a thriving organization, even more so at a struggling one. What better way to get his team communicating properly than by showing them step by step how great teams communicate?

Most executives quickly signed on. But a couple rebelled. Alan patiently explained that this was the way he'd chosen to run the meeting. He wasn't forcing the rebellious ones to follow his lead. "If you don't want to," he told them, "that's your choice. It doesn't make you a bad person. It just means you can't be part of the team." No yelling, no threats, no histrionics.

Alan's first days at Ford are a testament to how willfully—and predictably—people resist change. This was the same Ford leadership team responsible for posting a record $12.7 billion loss the year Alan arrived, the same team asking the new CEO to go hat in hand to bankers in New York and borrow $23 billion to keep Ford operating. If any group was ready for a change, it was Alan's team. Yet even with their jobs on the line, two of the executives were refusing to change their behavior in the BPR. It wasn't long before these two resisters decided to become former Ford executives.

Why would executives be willing to pull the rip cord on their careers rather than adapt to such a simple routine? My only interpretation is ego. In the same way that surgeons reject the simple proven structure of a checklist for washing their hands, many executives are too proud to admit they need structure. They consider repetitious activity as mundane, uncreative, somehow beneath them. How could something so simple do any good?

To Alan simple repetition was the key—in fact, the essential element in structure—particularly the color code that encouraged division heads to highlight concerns in yellow and problem areas in red. In the same way that Daily Questions drive us to measure our effort *every day* and then face the reality of our own behavior, the executives would be announcing how they graded themselves every Thursday—without deviation. Self-scoring, whether it was a letter grade or Alan's color coding, demanded transparency and honesty—what Alan called "visibility." It encouraged everyone to take responsibility, which had an unexpected power in a public forum of CEO and peers. Everyone in the room could see if progress was being made. And the process never ended. The executives knew they'd be meeting again the following week, and the week after that, and so on. And Alan and the entire team would be there, listening to all the reviews and helping one another make progress. Alan's message was impossible to miss. He was telling his team, "We know we will continue to make progress on our plan because we all know the real status, and we are positively committed to working together to accomplish the plan."

Alan's rigid format for the weekly meeting initially seemed

like a burden to some executives. The repetition. The preparation. The time spent. Slowly they began to appreciate that they were being handed a gift.

They weren't allowed to digress or stonewall or try end runs around painful subjects. They had to face the reality of Ford's dire situation. In making everyone repeat name, rank, priorities, and color-coded grading each week, Alan had given them a focused and purposefully narrow vocabulary. Everyone knew the plan. Everyone knew the status. Everyone knew the areas that needed special attention. This is how the executives discussed the only metric that mattered during Ford's turnaround: *How can we help one another more?*

That's one of structure's major contributions to any change process. It limits our options so that we're not thrown off course by externalities. If we're only allowed five minutes to speak, we find a way to make our case with a newfound concision—and it's usually a better speech because of the structural limitations (most audiences would agree).

Imposing structure on parts of our day is how we seize control of our otherwise unruly environment.

When we make a shopping list, we're imposing structure on our spending—to remember to buy what we need and avoid buying what we don't need.

When we follow a recipe we're relying on structure to simplify the complexity of cooking—and improve our odds of delivering an appealing dish.

When we formulate our bucket list we're imposing structure on the rest of our life.

When we join a reading group, we're imposing structure on our reading habits (and possibly restructuring our social life).

When we attend church every Sunday morning or track our weekly running mileage, we're using some form of structure to gain control of the wayward corners of our lives. We're telling ourselves, "In this area I need help." And structure provides the help.

Successful people know all this intuitively. Yet we discount structure when it comes to honing our interpersonal behavior. Structure is fine for organizing our calendar, or learning a technically difficult task, or managing other people, or improving a quantifiable skill. But for the simple tasks of interacting with other people we prefer to wing it—for reasons that sound like misguided variations on "I shouldn't need to do that."

We think "Plays well with others" is a category for grading schoolchildren, not grown-ups like us. We tell ourselves, *I'm a confident, successful adult. I shouldn't have to constantly monitor if I'm being nice or if people like me.*

Or we hold ourselves blameless for any interpersonal friction; it's always someone else's fault, not ours. *The other guy has to change. I shouldn't have to.*

Or we're so satisfied with how far our behavior has already taken us in life that we smugly reject any reason to change. *If it ain't broke, don't fix it.*

This is the payoff built into the core structural element of this book—the Daily Questions. Asking ourselves, "Did I do my best . . ." is another way of admitting, "In this area I need help." Answering the questions every day without fail is how we instill the rigor and discipline that have been missing from our lives. The net result is a clarity and unequivocality that makes us confront the question we try so hard to avoid: are we getting better?

Chapter 15

But It Has to Be the Right Structure

We do not get better without structure, whether we're targeting an organizational goal or a personal one. But it has to be structure that fits the situation and the personalities involved.

Alan Mulally brought his concept of organizational structure with him when he arrived at Ford. It was off-the-shelf structure, but it was his shelf. It mirrored his training and mindset as an engineer. It was a structure of zero tolerance—for personality clashes, for putting self above team, for any deviation from the rules. It worked for him and Ford spectacularly. But it wouldn't work in all settings.

Different people respond to different structure. I saw this clearly when I worked with Robert, the head of an East Coast insurance company. Robert's greatest asset was his large extroverted personality. He was the classic glad-handing, backslapping, high-energy salesman. Always on the go, always pursuing the next big deal. It had made him a record-breaking producer—practically a legend in company lore. He was respected, admired, and liked, which is one reason he eventually became CEO. The problem was a familiar one: a great salesman doesn't necessarily make a great leader, even one with a charismatic and outsized personality.

Formal 360-degree feedback was something new for Robert when we met to discuss the data. He joked that his direct reports might be too timid to give him the unvarnished truth.

"Not to worry," I said. "Excessively positive feedback will be the least of your concerns."

He said he wanted the bad news, so I gave it to him. "Your lowest score was on 'Provides clear goals and direction.' You're an eight percentile."

"Just to be clear, what does eight percentile mean?" he asked.

"It means that ninety-two percent of the leaders I've tracked in the company are better than you."

To his credit, Robert was a good sport and eager to get better. "It looks like we have work to do," he said. If he wasn't wearing a jacket at the time, I think he would have rolled up his sleeves to get started.

Robert's low scores on providing clear goals and direction indicated a chaotic management style. That wasn't surprising. As a gifted salesman, he relied on instinct, reading people, and knowing his customers. He'd never really developed his managerial muscles—paying attention to direct reports, mentoring them, following up on decisions and providing feedback, fine-tuning strategy as the business climate changed. He was so customer-centric, so focused on external rather than internal matters, one executive cited him for not calling enough meetings. I'd never heard an employee say, "We need *more* meetings."

Robert's challenge, as I saw it, was twofold: he had to change *himself* and his *environment* simultaneously—which meant aligning his team's behavior with his own. I had a simple off-the-shelf structure for him that had worked with clients many times before. It took the form of six basic questions. The questions weren't a big surprise to Robert—except for the fact that he'd never created the time or circumstance to pose them to himself and his people.

We solved that problem by immediately establishing a bi-monthly (every other month) one-on-one meeting format for Robert with each of his nine direct reports. It gave Robert a chance to display his new approach—to demonstrate that he was changing. Weekly meetings would have been too jarring a change. Every six months would have been too infrequent to make an impression. My only instruction to Robert was to be consistent. Like Alan Mulally repeating his lines, he had to stick to the script. The agenda for each meeting was a sheet of paper with the following questions:

- Where are we going?
- Where are you going?
- What is going well?
- Where can we improve?
- How can I help you?
- How can you help me?

Where are we going? tackled the big-picture priorities at the company. It forced Robert to articulate—not in his mind, but out loud so each executive could hear it personally—what he wanted for the company and what he was expecting from the executive. The details are not important here. The crucial fact is that Robert was describing a vision that could be discussed openly now, not merely guessed at. The back-and-forth dialogue was a first step in changing both the environment and Robert's reputation.

Where are you going? Robert then turned the table and asked each person to answer the same question about themselves, thus aligning *their* behavior and mindset with Robert's. In short order, they were replicating Robert's candor and honesty about their responsibilities and goals.

What is going well? Bad as he was at setting clear goals, Robert scored almost as low at providing constructive feedback. No meetings, no opportunities to praise his superstars. So the third portion of every meeting required him to openly recognize recent achievements by the executive facing him. Then he asked a question seldom asked by leaders: "What do you think that you and your part of the organization are doing well?" This wasn't just a compulsory upbeat moment in a meeting. It helped Robert learn about good news that he may otherwise have missed.

Where can we improve? This forced Robert to give his direct reports constructive suggestions for the future—something he'd rarely done and that his people didn't expect from him. Then he added a challenge: "If you were your own coach, what would you suggest for yourself?" The ideas he heard amazed him, largely because they were often better than his suggestions. He was okay with that. He was not only shaping the world around him, he was learning from it.

How can I help you? This is the most welcome phrase in any leader's repertoire. We can never say it enough, whether we're in the role of a parent or friend—or a busy CEO running a meeting. It has a reciprocal power few of us take advantage of. When we offer our help, we are nudging people to admit they need help. We are adding *needed* value, not interfering or imposing. That's what Robert was going for: building alignment between everyone's interests.

How can you help me? Asking for help means exposing our weaknesses and vulnerabilities—not an easy thing to do. Robert wanted to be a role-model CEO. By asking for ongoing help and focusing on his own improvement, he was encouraging everyone to do the same.

The improvements at Robert's company didn't happen overnight. But they never would have happened without some sort of structure. This simple structure played to Robert's strength. He had always been a great communicator with customers. Now he was deploying the same skill with employees.

In hindsight, the structure's biggest impact may have been to slow down Robert. Instead of always being on the go, he had to carve out serious time in his calendar for nine one-on-one meetings every two months.

Another key element in Robert's process was not just what he did every other month, but what each of his direct reports did in between the bimonthly sessions. In the same way that Alan Mulally involved each of his team members in the transformation of Ford, Robert involved his team in his own transformation toward becoming a better leader. Robert gave each team member carte blanche to call him on any leadership failing and to take personal responsibility for immediately contacting Robert if he or she felt confusion or ambiguity on direction, coaching, or feedback. Robert changed himself and his environment. Robert added structure. The team assumed responsibility. The combination produced amazing results.

When Robert retired four years later, his final 360-degree feedback report rated him a 98 percentile on "Provides clear goals and direction." What most amazed Robert was all the time he saved. He summed up: "I spent less time with my people when I was rated a 98 than I did when I was rated an 8. In the beginning, my team couldn't tell the difference between social 'chitchat' and goal clarity. By involving them in a simple structure, I could give them what they needed from me in a way that respected their time and mine."

That's an added value of matching structure with our desire to change. Structure not only increases our chance of success, it makes us more efficient at it.

Chapter 16

Behaving Under the Influence of Depletion

Has this ever happened to you?

- You come home after an intense decision-filled day at work. Your partner wants to lock in vacation plans. The two of you have discussed the basics—when and where you're going—but the details need to be settled. You say, "Whatever you decide is fine with me."

- You wake up later than usual with insufficient time for your morning workout. You tell yourself you'll hit the gym that evening after work. But at day's end, carrying your briefcase and gym bag from the office, you think, "I can skip today. I'll work out tomorrow morning."

- You arrive at your apartment after a grinding workday of back-to-back meetings and phone calls. It's early in the evening—a beautiful summer day with three hours of daylight left. You can take a walk. You can

call friends and arrange to meet up later. You can
cook yourself a nice meal. You can catch up on bills
or thank-you notes or emails. You can finish the book
you're reading. Instead you grab a bag of pretzels or
a Greek yogurt, turn on the TV, plop yourself on the
sofa, and mindlessly watch *The Shawshank Redemption*
for the thirty-eighth time—on basic cable with
commercial interruptions.

What's going on here? Why do our discipline and decisive-
ness fade at the end of the day, to the point where we opt
to do nothing instead of doing something enjoyable or useful? It's not because we're inherently weak. It's because we're
weakened.

The social psychologist Roy F. Baumeister coined the term
ego depletion in the 1990s to describe this phenomenon. He
contended that we possess a limited conceptual resource
called ego strength, which is depleted through the day by
our various efforts at self-regulation—resisting temptations,
making trade-offs, inhibiting our desires, controlling our
thoughts and statements, adhering to other people's rules.
People in this state, said Baumeister, are ego depleted.

Baumeister and other researchers have studied depletion
in myriad situations. At first, they studied self-control—our
conscious efforts to restrain an impulse in order to achieve a
goal or obey a rule—often by tempting people with chocolate.
They found that trying to resist a chocolate cookie lowered
people's ability to resist other temptations later on. Like fuel
in a gas tank, our self-control is finite and runs down with
steady use. By the end of the day, we're worn down and vulnerable to foolish choices.

Depletion isn't limited to self-control. It applies to many forms of self-regulated behavior.

Most obviously it affects our decision making. The more decisions we're obliged to make, whether it's choosing among the dozens of options when buying a new car or reducing the list of attendees at an off-site meeting, the more fatigued we get in handling subsequent decisions. Researchers call this *decision fatigue*, a state that leaves us with two courses of action: 1) we make careless choices or 2) we surrender to the status quo and do nothing. Decision fatigue is why the head-scratching purchases we make on Tuesday get returned on Wednesday; we're more clearheaded the next day when we're not depleted. It's also why we put off decisions; we're too drained to decide *now*.

A vivid real-life example of this appeared in a 2011 study of 1,100 decisions by an Israeli parole board. Researchers discovered that prisoners who appeared before the board early in the morning were granted parole 70 percent of the time while prisoners appearing late in the day were approved only 10 percent of the time. There was no meaningful pattern—no bias or malice among the three Israeli board members—except the time of day. The arduous work of deciding prisoners' fates all morning wore down the board members, so by the afternoon they chose the easy course of not deciding at all; they let 90 percent of prisoners finish their sentences.

Ego depletion has been cited to explain all sorts of consumer behavior, from why we seek and accept a waiter's recommendation (we're so depleted we'll let a stranger choose our food) to why impulse items such as candy bars and tiny bottles of 5-hour Energy are located at the checkout counter (retailers know that after making many decisions among the aisles customers are less likely to resist any temptation).

What interests me though is depletion's impact on our interpersonal behavior and our capacity to change. If shopping, deciding, and resisting temptation are depleting, then other behavioral challenges must be depleting, too (and research confirms this).

Dealing all day with difficult, high-maintenance colleagues is depleting. Maintaining a compliant façade around a leader you don't respect is depleting. Excessive multitasking is depleting. Trying to persuade people to agree with you when they are inclined to oppose you is depleting. So is trying to make people like you when they are predisposed to dislike you. Suppressing your opinions—or for that matter, engaging in any effort to control your emotions around others—is depleting.

Unlike being physically tired, however, we're usually unaware of depletion. It's not like engaging in strenuous physical activity where we expect to feel the weariness in our muscles—and take time out to rest. Depletion, like stress, is an invisible enemy. Until someone invents a body gauge to tell us we're running on emotional empty, we can't measure it, so we don't appreciate how it's grinding us down, affecting our behavioral discipline—and exposing us to bad judgment and undesirable actions.

It's one thing to engage in depleting activities, but there's another dimension: *How we behave under the influence of depletion.* Doing things that deplete us is not the same as doing things when we're depleted. The former is cause, the latter effect.

But the effect isn't pretty. Under depletion's influence we

are more prone to inappropriate social interactions, such as talking too much, sharing intimate personal information, and being arrogant. We are less likely to follow social norms; for example, we are more likely to cheat. We are less helpful. We can also be more aggressive; the effort of curbing our normal aggression depletes our self-control over that impulse. Conversely, we can also be more passive; when our intellectual resources are sapped, we are more easily persuaded by others and less adept at coming up with counterarguments.

Basically, all the natural urges we try to rein in during the day have the potential to rush toward center stage as the day progresses and our depletion increases. It doesn't mean they will materialize, but they're lurking within us, waiting for the right trigger.

One of this book's central arguments is that our environment affects us in powerful, insidious, and mysterious ways. Depletion is one of those environmental hazards. I don't want to overstate depletion's impact, or make it sound as if we are all emotional time bombs ready to explode the moment our so-called ego strength drains down to empty. Like Hans Selye's discovery of stress in 1936 (it's easy to forget there was a time when doctors were oblivious to the connection between stress—the body's response to any demand—and disease), depletion is a way of seeing the world anew and appreciating the demands placed on us by our constant efforts at self-regulation.

Once our eyes are opened, new courses of action immediately come to mind. Most obviously, we can start tracking our days in terms of depletion. We can't measure or quantify our depletion—we're not even aware of it—but we can assemble a useful list of what is or isn't depleting. A day at the beach—no hassles, no worries except applying SPF 30—is probably low depletion. So is recreational hiking all day in the mountains, despite the physical demands. The many things we do by choice, from painting a kid's room to visiting a friend in the hospital, are usually low depletion.

On the other hand, spending a big part of our day on the phone with customer service, heroically straining to remain polite as we fail to locate a missing package or correct a billing error, is probably high depletion. Biting our tongue when we hear the idiocies spouted by our brother-in-law or neighbor is high depletion. Any effort to contain our normal impulses in the face of other people's obstinacy can be high depletion. It builds up incrementally, so that by day's end we are not functioning at our best. When other people call us out for disappointing or upsetting them, we apologize by saying "I had a rough day," or "I'm exhausted." That's as close as we come to appreciating that we are depleted.

Codifying our depleting events provides a clearer picture of how altered we may be at day's end, how diminished in terms of willpower. Like monitoring our alcohol intake if we have to drive, we're aware if we're acting under the influence of depletion. And that bit of self-knowledge reveals where the risks are.

Making big decisions late in the day is an obvious risk. Thus, instead of meeting with your financial adviser after work to decide where your money goes—when you're literally SWI, spending while impaired—make it the first depleting event in your day, when you're deciding with a full tank.

Coming home after work to a frenetic family household can be risky, too. If you've ever walked in the door and snapped at your family because the toys are on the floor, or the den is a mess, or the dog needs walking—the triggering irritant is irrelevant—you know depletion's power. You had the option of being happy to see your family or making everyone miserable. Running low on willpower, you made the wrong choice.

Structure is how we overcome depletion. In an almost magical way, structure slows down how fast our discipline and self-control disappear. When we have structure, we don't have to make as many choices; we just follow the plan. And the net result is we're not being depleted as quickly.

Alan Mulally must have known this intuitively with his highly structured Thursday BPR meetings. High-achieving, headstrong executives have many behavioral choices in a meeting: What they say, whom they challenge or interrupt, in what terms they report progress, what they omit, how much cooperation or surliness they want to display. The choices, even in a meeting with familiar colleagues, are mind-numbing. Alan's structure took all of those choices off the table—and in doing so protected the Ford team from themselves. The BPR meetings started at 8 a.m. and often lasted several hours. If executives had been allowed to freewheel for so much time, their collective depletion in the last hour would have been palpable. Being handcuffed by Alan's rules minimized the depletion, kept them fresh and at their best with a full tank—and they didn't even know it.

If we provide ourselves with enough structure, we don't need discipline. The structure provides it for us. We can't structure everything obviously—no environment is *that* cooperative—but all of us rely on structure in small ways some of the time.

For example, the seven-day pillbox is a structural godsend for the millions of Americans who take daily prescription medication. It solves a major challenge in the doctor-patient relationship: patient compliance. We wake up on a Thursday, ingest the contents of the "Th" slot, and achieve compliance with little effort. We regard the pillbox as a convenience but on another level, it's a structural surrogate for self-discipline. We don't have to remember to take our pills. The pillbox does the remembering for us.

We're probably not aware of how much depletion-fighting structure we've injected into our lives. When we follow an unshakable wake-up routine, or write down an agenda for our meetings, or stop at the same coffee shop before work, or clear our messy desk before opening up the laptop to write, we're surrendering to our routine, and burning up less energy trying to be disciplined. Our routine has taken care of that.

I can't have enough structure in my day. I only wear khaki pants and green polo shirts to work (to add discipline to my shaky fashion sense). I pay a woman to call me with my Daily Questions (to discipline my self-awareness). I delegate all travel decisions to an assistant and never question her choices (to discipline my time). It's an irresistible equation: the more structure I have, the less I have to worry about. The peace of mind more than compensates for whatever I sacrifice in autonomy.

I appreciate that not everyone is as eager to cede control of their lives as I am. Some people are mavericks. They chafe at the imposition of any rule or routine, as if their self-generated discipline is morally and aesthetically superior to externally generated discipline. I get it. We like our freedom. But when I consider the behavioral edge that structure provides, my only question is: *Why would anyone say no to a little more structure?*

Chapter 17

We Need Help When
We're Least Likely to Get It

At the intersection where structure and behavior bump up against each other, there's a paradox. We rely on structure to govern the predictable parts of our lives. We know the places we're obligated to be, the tasks we're paid to do, the people we'll be meeting soon. They're in our calendars and in our heads so we can prepare. We have structure—etiquette, our rules for what's appropriate—to guide and instruct us. We generally know how to behave when we see something coming.

But what about all the unguarded interpersonal moments that aren't marked down on our schedules? The annoying colleague, noisy neighbor, rude customer, angry client, distressed child, or disappointed spouse who unexpectedly demand attention when we're neither prepared nor in the best shape to respond well? If the moment materializes at the wrong time of day, we may be operating under depletion's influence—and regret it.

That's the paradox: *We need help when we're least likely to get it.*

Our environment is loaded with surprises that trigger odd, unfamiliar responses from us. We end up behaving against our interests. Quite often, we don't even realize it. We lack the structural tools to handle bewildering interpersonal challenges. (If only there were an app for that—a ringing tone on our smartphone alerting us, *Things are about to get testy. Be cool.*)

I recall some years ago when my friend Derek unexpectedly lost his fifty-nine-year-old father after a routine surgical procedure. The death hit Derek hard but after a week off to comfort his mother and settle estate matters, he went back to work, looking like the old Derek. During the next six months, however, he endured an unprecedented string of career calamities. His two biggest clients left him. A couple of valued employees jumped to the competition. And two projects were canceled. It took him three years to regroup and recover the income and status he'd lost.

When I asked him about that black hole in his career, Derek said, "It's a simple story. My father was the first person I loved who died. I was in shock. So I behaved like a man in shock. I neglected people that mattered. I ignored deadlines. I didn't return phone calls. People quickly chose to stop doing business with me. I see it now but only because of the damage I did to myself."

Derek is not rationalizing or making excuses. He was a consummate professional before that dark period, and has been since. The sloppy work habits were triggered by his father's sudden death—and his inability to deal with his grief. Society provides structure to deal with a loved one's passing—

funerals, mourning periods, grief counselors, support groups, therapists explaining Kübler-Ross's five stages of grief. But Derek either scoffed at or didn't have access to this kind of therapeutic structure. He only appreciated his dilemma after the fact. When he needed help, he made sure he wouldn't get it.

The Awful Meeting

Let's take it down a few notches in severity from the triggering impact of a parent's unexpected death and talk about more common interpersonal challenges where we respond poorly without structure. What kind of structure are we talking about?

It should be a simple structure that (a) *anticipates* that our environment will take a shot at us and (b) *triggers* a smart, productive response rather than foolish behavior. I suggest that simple structure is a variation on the Daily Questions, a process that requires us to score our effort and reminds us to be self-vigilant. It's a structure that alters our awareness profoundly.

For example, imagine that you have to go to a one-hour meeting that will be pointless, boring, a time-suck better spent catching up on your "real" work. (We've all been there.) You have no interest in masking how you feel about the meeting. You walk in sporting a sullen look on your face, signaling that you'd rather be anywhere but here. You slouch in your chair, resisting eye contact, doodling on a notepad, speaking only when you're called on, making perfunctory contributions. At meeting's end, you're the first one out the door. Your goal was to spend the hour being miserable—and you succeeded.

Now imagine at meeting's end you will be tested—just you—with four simple questions about how you spent that hour:

1. Did I do my best to be happy?
2. Did I do my best to find meaning?
3. Did I do my best to build positive relationships?
4. Did I do my best to be fully engaged?

If you knew that you were going to be tested, what would you do differently to raise your score on any of these four items?

I've posed this question to thousands of executives. Some typical responses:

- I would go into the meeting with a positive attitude.
- Instead of waiting for someone to make it interesting, I'd make it interesting myself.
- I'd try to help the presenter in some way instead of critiquing him in my head.
- I would come prepared with good questions.
- I would challenge myself to learn something meaningful in the meeting.
- I would try to build a positive relationship with someone in the room.
- I would pay attention and put away my smartphone.

Everyone has good answers. That's the motivational kicker in knowing you'll be tested afterward. It turns the indifferent environment of a boring meeting into a keen competition with yourself. It makes you hyperaware of your behavior. The specter of testing triggers a natural desire to achieve something that reflects well on you, that is, scoring well on happiness, meaning, engagement, and relationship building. Achieving misery falls by the wayside, exposed as the folly it is.

Here's my radical suggestion. From now on, pretend that you are going to be tested at every meeting! Your heart and mind will thank you for it. The hour that you spend in the meeting is one hour of your life that you never get back. If you are miserable, it is your misery, not the company's or your co-workers'. Why waste that hour being disengaged and cynical? By taking personal responsibility for your own engagement, you make a positive contribution to your company—and begin creating a better you.

Think of this idea as a small mental gyration for altering your behavior. Testing is usually a post hoc event—after the performance, then the scoring. This pretend-you'll-be-tested concept flips it around. It's not cheating. It's not a gimmick. It's structure, the kind that successful people already rely on. Like trial lawyers never asking a question they don't know the answer to, you're taking a test with the correct answers provided in advance—by you. For the one hour you find yourself in that dreaded meeting, you're giving yourself help when you need it most.

Chapter 18

Hourly Questions

Why stop at one hour? Why can't we string one hour into another and then another so that self-testing for an entire day becomes our structure?

In any situation we can live in one of three dimensions: past, present, or future. When we commit to being miserable in a dull meeting, we're doing one of two things, neither good:

1. We're wallowing in the past, remembering with regret and frustration all the previous boring meetings we've attended, or
2. We're thinking about the future, muddling through the meeting with impatience or misguided longing for whatever's next.

When we know we'll be tested—even if it's just pretend—we're forcing ourselves to live in the present. We're alert, aware, and mindful of our behavior and everyone else's, because we sense that in the very immediate future we will have to account for our actions. The present is the ideal place to be. This is where we shape ourselves into a better person. We can't do it in the past; that's gone. We can't do it in a future that exists only in our minds, where the people who matter have yet to arrive. We can only do it in the moment.

Adapting Daily Questions into Hourly Questions creates a powerful structure for locating ourselves in the moment.

Remember Griffin with the Clinking Cubes Problem from Chapter 12? A year after he solved that problem, Griffin came to me with another issue. Griffin lived in New York City but owned a weekend home in a lake community in New Hampshire, where over the years he and his wife had become good friends with several neighbors, all native New Englanders. On the rare occasions when these New Hampshire neighbors visited Manhattan, Griffin extended an open invitation to stay with him and his wife in their Upper West Side town house. Griffin's three grown children were out of the house, so there was plenty of room for overnight visitors to stay without being bothersome. Griffin enjoyed being a magnanimous host—until an unforeseen issue arose. Here's how Griffin explained it:

"In New Hampshire we socialize a lot with our neighbors. That's what everyone does on the lake. So we looked forward to seeing them in New York. They're hardy New Englanders, not city people. They don't visit New York that often. But after the third couple stayed with us, it got to be tiresome taking them around, repeating the same tour of the city's greatest hits: the Statue of Liberty, the 9/11 site and MoMA and the Museum of Natural History. We'd walk the High Line and Soho and Brooklyn, see a musical, eat at fancy restaurants. New York's our home base, so when we go to a Broadway show or museum it's because we want to, not because we're in the big city for a few days and want to squeeze everything in. I got grumpy with the last visitors, not where it ruptured a friendship but enough for my wife to mention it."

Another couple would soon be visiting Griffin for a three-day weekend and he was worried that as the visit stretched out, he'd ruin their time by betraying his real feelings. (In depletion terms, the effort of controlling himself would wear down his discipline—and he'd turn nasty.) He was frustrated with a situation of his own creation. The longer the guests stayed, the more the kind invitation he'd extended morphed into an intrusion. His situation was not much different than the prospect of the awful meeting. How do you transform an environment you dread into a positive experience?

Griffin was disciplined about self-testing. He believed in Daily Questions.

"Turn daily into hourly," I said. "When your New Hampshire friends are with you, test how you're holding up every hour with a few pointed questions."

"Only one question matters," he said. "Did I do my best to enjoy my friends?"

When the friends appeared, Griffin was ready. His Hourly Question provided a structure to guide his behavior, keep him on point. Thus, as he jostled with crowds at a trendy pizzeria in Bushwick or waited in line at the American Museum of Natural History Hayden Planetarium for the third time in six months, Griffin's smartphone, which he had set to vibrate at the top of the hour, reminded him to ponder the simple question: *Am I doing my best to enjoy my friends?* This continued throughout the day. He could either pass the hourly test or fail. Here's his report on a ten-hour day touring New York City:

"I expected it would be like a marathon. I'd pace myself,

starting out strong and barely standing at the finish line. That's when the hourly questioning would save me—when I was really frustrated and hating the situation. That's not what happened. After three or four hours, I got stronger, not weaker. The phone would vibrate, I'd review my behavior, congratulate myself for doing well, and get on with it. By the end of the day, when I expected to be at my most curmudgeonly, I was on cruise control. It was a great day."

Griffin's story seems to defy the notion of depletion. But it makes sense to me. Knowing he'd be tested hourly—and wanting to do well—meant Griffin didn't have a choice about enjoying himself (or else he'd fail a test he'd written!). The structure took being a curmudgeon out of the mix. No choice, no discipline required, no depletion.

One other thing: when we decide to behave well and our first steps are successful, we often achieve a self-fulfilling momentum—Griffin called it "cruise control"—where we don't have to try as hard to be good. Like getting through the first four days of a strict diet, if we can handle the initial stages of inhibiting our undesirable impulses, we're less likely to backslide. We don't want to waste the gains of our behavioral investment. Good behavior becomes the sunk cost we hate to sacrifice.

Can it be that simple? Evidently yes. The simpler the structure, the more likely we'll stick with it. And Hourly Questions are fairly simple, comprising a series of steps that segue so smoothly from one to the other we barely register them as discrete stages in the process:

1. *Pre-awareness.* Successful people are generally good at anticipating environments where their best behavior is

at risk. They're rarely ambushed by a tough negotiation, awful meeting, challenging confrontation. They know what they're getting into before they walk into the room. For lack of a better term, I call it pre-mindfulness— that sense, like an athlete mentally gearing up in the locker room before heading out onto the field, that a hyperaware mindset will soon be required.

2. *Commitment.* Successful people aren't wishy-washy about a course of action. Choosing Hourly Questions as a structure and articulating the specific questions is a commitment device—certainly better than *hoping* things will work out. It's the difference between considering a goal and writing it down.

3. *Awareness.* We're most vulnerable to our environment's whims when we ignore its impact on us. Hourly Questions, impinging on our consciousness with precise regularity, neutralize the ignorance and make us vibrantly aware. We don't have time to forget our situation or get distracted from our objective—because the next test is coming in sixty minutes.

4. *Scoring.* Grading our performance adds reflection to mindfulness. It's a force multiplier for awareness. It's one thing to do a task privately, another to do it while being watched by a supervisor. We're more self-conscious when we're being observed and judged— except now we are observing and judging ourselves.

5. *Repetition.* The best part of Hourly Questions is their rinse-and-repeat frequency. If we score poorly in one hourly segment, we get a chance to do better an hour later. A behavioral mulligan is built into the structure.

Hourly Questions have a specific short-term utility. It would be impractical and exhausting—and no doubt depleting—to rely on them for long-term behavioral challenges such as rebranding yourself as a nicer person. Despite the acute self-awareness that being nice requires, daily and weekly checkups are more than enough for a goal that rewards persistence and consistency. You answer your Daily Questions each night and gradually reap the benefit many months later. It's not an overnight religious conversion. You're playing a long game.

Hourly Questions are for the short game—when we require a burst of discipline to restrain our behavioral impulses for a defined period of time. Two universal situations come to mind:

There's the *dreaded event*—not just an awful meeting or weekend with houseguests but any environment where our inherent pessimism *going in* can trigger our careless unappealing behavior *during* the event. It could be the contrived camaraderie of a company retreat, or a tense Thanksgiving with the extended family, or a disappointing parent-teacher conference at a child's school. If we participate in these moments without a structure to discipline what we say and do, our pessimism becomes a self-fulfilling prophecy; we're crafting the unpleasantness we anticipated. Hourly Questions are one kind of structure to defuse pessimism. It's our choice.

Then there are *people*—the ones who throw us off our game because of their personalities and actions. It could be the colleague with the high chirping voice, or the customer service representative repeating the same nonhelpful response in six different ways, or the pompous know-it-all on the local school board, or the supermarket shopper in front of you with twenty items in the ten-item express line. We've seen these people before. And yet we still allow them to unhinge us. In those brief moments when we are vulnerable to the obtuseness and intransigence of another human being, Hourly Questions can bring out a newfound restraint in us.

Here's an irony: I don't rely on Hourly Questions for dreaded events and annoying people. Quite the opposite. My challenge is dealing with *events I'm really looking forward to* and *people I really enjoy.*

Consider, for example, the prospect of dinner at a top-flight restaurant with ten of my favorite clients. I don't know many people who would dread this event—and neither do I. My challenge in such an environment is a matter of excessive enjoyment and appetite control. Under the best of circumstances, I need help restraining myself around the temptations of the table (I'm not alone in this weakness). But in a festive atmosphere with terrific people, I'm even more vulnerable. The situation is custom-made for abandoned discipline and overindulgence. It takes place at the end of the day, when depletion is greatest. The food and drink are plentiful, creating opportunity. Everyone around me is in a jolly mood, which amps up my own jolliness and further reduces self-control. Life is good, I tell myself, so why not enjoy the moment and regret it later? It's a combustible environment for me. I become living proof that we need help when we are least likely to get it.

This is where Hourly Questions come to the rescue. I know I'm vulnerable in these situations, so I arm myself with as much structure as I can think of. I tell myself that I won't eat the wonderful dessert. Sometimes I make a pact with the person sitting next to me: neither of us will succumb to the temptation of dessert. Sometimes, like Odysseus putting wax in his sailors' ears, I ask the waitstaff to ignore me if I attempt to order dessert. But the most important structural element remains: I test myself every hour with the question: *Did I do my best to enjoy who is here rather than what is being served?*

I don't always grade out summa cum laude. Some evenings I eat the dessert anyway. But I don't forget to test myself hourly, and doing so reminds me that I am not an unconscious victim of my environment. Whatever I do, I'm indulging in a conscious choice, with eyes wide open. Even when I give myself middling grades, that heightened awareness is a net gain. The more I rely on this kind of self-testing for acute situations, the stronger my awareness, until it's a permanent part of who I am. That's a meaningful and lasting change I can live with.

Chapter 19

The Trouble with "Good Enough"

There are no absolutes in behavioral change. We never achieve perfect patience or generosity or empathy or humility (you pick the virtue).

It's nothing to be ashamed of. The best we can hope for is a consistency in our effort—a persistence of striving—that makes other people more charitable about our shortcomings.

For example, your normally punctual friend is late for a lunch date. She finally arrives, apologizing profusely for keeping you waiting. Do you hold it against her, marking it down as a major demerit in your relationship? Or do you forgive her, remembering that being late is so unlike her? I suspect, like most people, you opt for forgiveness.

You award her a reputation for punctuality *because of* rather than *despite* this one occasion of tardiness. A solitary lapse makes the virtue and her striving stand out in sharp relief. You'd expect the same if the tables were turned. You know that there's no such thing as a *fully* deserved reputation, not even among the most saintly among us. We all mess up once in a while.

What's worrisome is when the striving stops, our lapses become more frequent, and we begin to coast on our reputation. That's the perilous moment when we start to settle for "good enough."

Good enough isn't necessarily a bad thing. In many areas of life, chasing perfection is a fool's errand, or at least a poor use of our time. We don't need to spend hours taste-testing every mustard on the gourmet shelf to find the absolute best; a good enough brand will suffice for our sandwich.

For most things we suspend our hypercritical faculties and find satisfaction with the merely good. The economist Herbert Simon called this "satisficing"—our tendency to commodify everyday choices because chasing that last bit of improvement is not worth the time or effort. It will not significantly increase our happiness or satisfaction.

We do this with our choice of toothpaste, or detergent, or romance novels, or Japanese takeout.

We do it with seemingly critical choices such as where we bank or which credit card we use. Likewise, with our accountants and lawyers, even our dentists and ophthalmologists and GPs. We make these choices randomly, not based on a systematic search for best in class.

I dare say we even settle for good enough in choosing where to live. Everyone gripes about the weather but if perfect climate really mattered we'd all live in San Diego (America's most reliable weather) or Boulder, Colorado (310 sunny days a year). Even in choosing our environment the vast majority of us settle for good enough.

We get a little more picky when our self-esteem is at stake

(such as deciding where to apply to college) or our survival hangs in the balance (such as picking a neurosurgeon). But considering that less than 2 percent of us apply to the top one hundred colleges and that second-tier surgeons have a steady supply of patients, too, even in these big decisions we settle for good enough—and it usually works out fine. Our lives aren't destroyed because Yale rejected us or our surgeon hasn't won a Nobel Prize in medicine.

The problem begins when this good enough attitude spills beyond our marketplace choices and into the things we say and do.

The mustard on a sandwich can be good enough. But in the interpersonal realm—we're talking about how a husband treats his wife, or a son deals with an aging parent, or a trusted friend responds when people are counting on him— good enough is setting the bar too low. Satisficing is not an option. It neither satisfies nor suffices. It disappoints people, creates distress where there should be harmony, and taken to extremes, ends up destroying relationships.

Let's look at four environments that trigger good enough behavior.

1. When our motivation is marginal

In many ways this book is for people with marginal motivation. Normal human beings, like me and the people I coach. Probably you, too. In theory, fully motivated people don't need help finding the discipline and structure to get things done, including changing for the better. Good enough is not in their vocabulary.

We know what high motivation looks like. Anyone who's attended a fancy wedding has seen it. For sheer obsessiveness, attention to detail, a refusal to accept good enough, and the willpower to fit into a wedding dress two sizes smaller than usual, nothing tops the motivation of a bride preparing for her wedding day. (Think Michael Phelps's motivation while training for his eight gold medals at the Beijing Olympics. Then double it.) If we could bottle that energy, there would be no need for chapters titled "The Trouble with 'Good Enough.'"

We immediately recognize that level of motivation in the (even slightly) extraordinary effort of others—say, an assistant staying late while we're heading home or our child going straight to her room to tackle homework rather than plop in front of the TV. We note it and admire it—because it's inspiring to see people spurning the seductive pull of good enough.

We also know what marginal motivation looks like, although we're less alert to it in ourselves. It's all those moments when our enthusiasm for a task is dulled or compromised and we're vulnerable to mediocrity.

Skill is the beating heart of high motivation. The more skill we have for the task at hand, the easier it is to do a good job. The easier to do a good job, the more we enjoy it. The more we enjoy it, the higher our motivation to continue doing it, even if the task is mentally exhausting (like solving a thorny technical problem) or physically grueling (like swimming endless laps at top speed) or dangerous (like rock climbing). If we're great at it, we'll jump into it despite the costs and risks.

It makes sense that we are highly motivated to do things we're good at. Good performance provides good feedback, placing us in a constantly reinforcing feedback loop. If we're winning big at the poker table, we keep playing. Our rising stack of chips is unequivocal feedback telling us to remain in our seat.

But we often overlook the flip side—the situations when insufficient skill practically preordains our marginal motivation. We miss the direct connection between low skill and low enthusiasm until someone points it out to us.

I once asked a CEO client, "What would make you happy?"

"To be better at golf," he said without hesitation.

I don't know what I was expecting him to say—something profound about world peace or ending hunger—but he wasn't my first high-achieving client obsessed with golf.

"Are you any good?" I asked.

"Not really. I don't embarrass myself out there, but I never improve."

"How old are you?" I asked.

"Fifty-eight."

"Were you a good athlete in high school?" I continued.

"Mediocre at best. I was on the swim team."

"Do you enjoy practicing?"

"I'd rather go out with friends and just play."

"So, you're over fifty, an age when no athlete in history has gotten better than he or she was before fifty. You don't claim much eye-hand coordination, so you lack the innate skill for the game. And you hate to practice, which I understand is crucial to improvement. Does that sum up your situation?"

He nodded.

"My advice is to enjoy the game and quit worrying about getting better. Better golf is not in your future."

I basically told him to settle for good enough—which may

sound like a contradiction of this entire chapter except for one significant factor: when our lack of skill at any task dramatically reduces our motivation to do that task, defaulting to some form of good enough is a shrewd option. It's not ideal, but it's better than kidding ourselves—or misleading others into expecting a full-throated performance and disappointing them with something marginal. Marginal motivation produces a marginal outcome. (It's amazing this insight still surprises us.)

We also underestimate how the quality of our goals affects our motivation. We fail at New Year's resolutions because our goals are almost always about marginal stuff, which we pursue with marginal motivation. Instead of aiming at core issues—say, escaping a hateful job—we aim for vague, amorphous targets like "take a class" or "travel more." A marginal goal begets marginal effort.

Finally, we don't appreciate how quickly our motivation can turn marginal at the first signs of progress. This is the invisible lure of good enough feeding upon itself. I see this sometimes with my one-on-one clients. They start out with high motivation and then shift down after six to eight months of steady progress on their interpersonal goals. They think they've "solved" the problem and can quit focusing so hard on relationships.

It's my job to tell them that their glimpse of the finish line is a mirage. They don't get to determine if they're better. The people around them make that call. When that reality sinks in, their motivation recharges and we get back to work.

The takeaway: If your motivation for a task or goal is in any way compromised—because you lack the skill, or don't take the

*task seriously, or think what you've done so far is good enough—
don't take it on. Find something else to show the world how much
you care, not how little.*

2. When we're working pro bono

I've already established my admiration for Frances Hesselbein. But one moment in her career sticks out above everything else as behavior worth modeling:

A few years ago, Frances got an invitation to the White
House. The White House date conflicted with her commitment to speak to a small nonprofit group in Denver. To most
people this wouldn't be a conundrum: *A meeting with the president of the United States or an unpaid speech in Denver?* We call
the folks in Denver, explain the situation, offer to reschedule
or promise to come back the next year. After all, it's pro bono.
We're doing the folks in Denver a favor. They'll understand.

Frances went the other way. She told the White House
she wouldn't be attending. "I have a commitment," she said.
"They're expecting me." (The real kicker for me, the cherry
on top of this integrity sundae: Frances never told the Denver
group about the White House invitation.)

Most of us believe we'd do the high-integrity thing
like Frances Hesselbein, but experience suggests otherwise.
When we find ourselves in a position where we have an excuse to do less than our best, how many of us grab the pro
bono excuse as a lifeline?

By pro bono, I don't just mean that we're not getting paid
for our expertise (like high-powered lawyers representing

nonprofit organizations for free) but rather any voluntary activity that's a personal choice—whether it's coaching our kid's soccer team or washing dishes at a soup kitchen or mentoring at-risk teens at the local high school or agreeing to give a speech. We create casual equivalencies between volunteering and our level of commitment. We think that because we raised our hand to *help out* we can raise our hand to *opt out* at the inconvenient moments. This is how our fine and noble intentions degrade into good enough outcomes. This is how our integrity gets compromised.

Integrity is an all-or-nothing virtue (like being half pregnant, there's no such thing as semi-integrity). We need to display it whatever obligations we've made. We don't need integrity to live up to our smart commitments—the ones where there's an obvious payoff for showing up and doing our best. The true test is delivering top-shelf performance with our stupid commitments—the kind we didn't want to do in the first place and got talked into. We know this is the right thing to do, but caught up in a challenging environment—we're tired or overextended, we have better options, it costs more than we thought, the White House is calling with a more glamorous offer—we think more about our situation than the people counting on us.

The takeaway: Pro bono is an adjective, not an excuse. If you think doing folks a favor justifies doing less than your best, you're not doing anyone any favors, including yourself. People forget your promise, remember your performance. It's like a restaurant donating food to a homeless shelter, but delivering shelf-dated leftovers and scraps that hungry people can barely swallow. The restaurant owner thinks he's being generous, that any donation is better than nothing. Better than nothing is not even close to good enough—and good enough, after we make a promise, is never good enough.

3. When we behave like "amateurs"

After working for a year with my client Dennis, I'd heard amazing reports about his progress. His issue was the most common problem for high-achieving C-level executives: an overwhelming need to win. When I first met Dennis, this manifested itself in a combative verbal style, where he was always the prosecutor putting peers and direct reports on the defensive. He didn't do it with the CEO or with important customers, which added the distasteful qualities of hypocrisy and sycophancy to Dennis's win-at-all-costs reputation.

Dennis got better quickly (his need to win, applied to getting better rather than humiliating co-workers, surely helped). But he wasn't happy. In our regular phone check-ins, he was always complaining about his wife. It wasn't chivalrous of him, but it sounded as if they argued from the moment he came home in the evening to the moment he left for work the next morning. The office had become a sanctuary for him. Home—a house in the suburbs with three young children— was a marital war zone.

I don't usually get involved with a client's domestic issues but the disparity between Dennis's new work behavior— courtesy, tolerance, thinking before he spoke—and what he was describing at home was hard to ignore. I'd seen him turn into a man of Zen-like patience over the year. He had become an expert at employing AIWATT before speaking. He didn't

have to assert his dominance in every situation. He gladly suffered the occasional fool. But not at home, apparently.

The next time we met in person, I asked him about it. Why
did his work environment bring out his best behavior while
home triggered the old Dennis?

"At work I have to be professional," he said. "Your feedback taught me that."

"And what about home?" I asked. "It's okay to be an amateur with your family?"

That stumped Dennis into speechlessness. I'd hit a nerve.
Tears were welling up in his eyes. I didn't mean it harshly.
When Dennis used the term *professional* it explained a lot of
the discordant behavior I'd seen in others over the years. Who
among us hasn't noticed how in our home environment we
behave in ways we'd never tolerate in a work environment?
Some of it is goofy harmless stuff like being absent-minded
and mechanically incompetent. Other behavior is more dis-
tressing; we're brooding, taciturn, isolated, antisocial, or
angry. Careers collapse if we bring such behavior from home
to the workplace. So for the most part, we don't.

It's easy to see why. At work, we have all sorts of structures in place to maintain our professional poise—formal
ones like performance reviews and regular meetings, infor-
mal ones like online gossip and water-cooler chatter. There's
also the powerful motivator of money, status, power—and
keeping our job.

At home—whether we live alone or have a family—the
structures and motivators vanish. We're free to be anyone we
want to be. And we don't always aim high enough.

That's what got to Dennis. A professional shoots for the
highest standards. An amateur settles for good enough. He'd

worked so hard to be a better person at work but never bothered to extend the effort to his wife and children, people who presumably mattered to him more than his co-workers. The thought of being an amateur husband or father was hard for Dennis to accept. It wasn't the person he wanted to be. Hence the tears.

Most of us fall into this amateur-versus-professional trap each day without knowing it. And not just when we switch between home and work. We switch between amateur and professional on the job, too, usually in areas that don't reflect who we think we are.

I remember giving a talk at a corporate retreat for a health-care company. The CEO spoke before me for forty-five minutes. He wasn't very good. He read the speech (written by a staffer), clicked to several slides on the screen, rarely looked up to see if anyone was paying attention, never altered his tone or tried to perk up his audience with an ad-libbed remark. He wasn't a hard act to follow and (how do I express this modestly?) I rocked the house. I prowled the stage, mingled with the audience, got people moving around and answering questions, laughing and high-fiving one another. My usual response. This is what I do for a living. I cared. I tried. It showed.

Afterward, the CEO rewarded me with a left-handed compliment. He said he enjoyed my performance, then added, "But you're a professional speaker. I can see why you're better at it than I am."

He was telling me that giving a speech wasn't part of his real job as CEO. He'd segregated that duty from his other responsibilities. As CEO he considered himself a total professional. As a speaker, he was a self-designated amateur, content with good enough (and frankly, he didn't rise to that level). He'd programmed himself for mediocrity.

We all do it. We segregate the parts we're good at from the parts we're not—and treat our strengths as the real us. The weaknesses are an aberration; they belong to a stranger, someone we refuse to acknowledge as us. This is how we confer amateur status on ourselves and secure our license for good enough.

The takeaway: We are professionals at what we do, amateurs at what we want to become. We need to erase this devious distinction—or at least close the gap between professional and amateur—to become the person we want to be. Being good over here does not excuse being not so good over there.

4. When we have compliance issues

People have compliance issues for two reasons: either they think they have a better way of doing something (classic need-to-win syndrome) or they're unwilling to commit fully when it means obeying someone else's rules of behavior (classic not-invented-here syndrome). Such orneriness often degrades the situation instead of making it better.

Nowhere are compliance issues more obvious than in the doctor-patient relationship.

For example, a few years ago, Richard, one of my coaching associates, underwent triple-bypass heart surgery. The operation was a success. As part of his recovery, Richard worked out a weight loss program with his doctor to shed some of the forty-five pounds he'd gained in the two decades since college. Twenty-five pounds was the target they agreed on—nothing extreme or unrealistic. The diet plan was gentle—portion control, reduce carbs and cheese, increase fresh fruit and vegetables, coupled with a daily forty-minute walk. Richard lost twelve pounds quickly, then plateaued, then gradually regained a couple of pounds. And that's where he remains today, still in his mid-forties and settling for half measures instead of going all out to stay alive. This wasn't the same as you or I failing to lose the proverbial "last ten pounds"— the vanity pounds that are so hard to shed because our body likes them. Richard's weight loss wasn't about vanity. It was triggered by a serious cardiac event. His health depended on compliance with the program. Yet he still stopped halfway and went no further. Losing twelve pounds, he decided, was good enough.*

We all have compliance issues, admitted or not. We all resist being told how to behave, even when it's for our own good or we know our failure to comply will hurt someone.

---

*I've often wondered why doctors let patients get away with this misbehavior. Doctors know compliance is a major issue—that a reported 30 percent of patients do not take their medicine for a life-threatening disease. Yet they do little about it. It's as if the medical community believes their responsibility ends when the patient leaves the office. When was the last time your doctor called or emailed to ask if you were complying with the recommended treatment? This is precisely where a little structure and follow-up—a lot like Daily Questions—could help patients become more engaged in their health. Doctors already remind us via phone or text us about upcoming appointments (because it's in their interest to reduce cancellations). They have the technology, with no additional human labor, to follow up on patient compliance. Private enterprise knows this already. There are more than a dozen "medicine adherence" apps that can ping us daily to take our pills. Of course, this assumes something will trigger us to download the app. Our doctor's involvement might improve the odds. Thus endeth my editorial on the matter.

- A friend shares a secret with the caveat that it's strictly between us—and despite our promise to tell no one, we make a "good enough" exception for our spouse. The friend, we tell ourselves, surely didn't mean for us to keep something from the person we live with.

- Our child breaks something valuable. Before admitting to the accident, the child makes us promise not to get angry. We contain our anger for the moment, but we carry it with us for days, taking it out on the child in indirect ways.

- A customer expects daily updates on a project but when there's nothing new to report, we skip a day or two. Without telling the other party, we unilaterally rewrite the tacit agreement between us to touch base every day, no matter what. We opt for good enough— and needlessly confuse our customer.

These are three random examples from our hundreds of small daily acts of disobedience and letting people down. Most of us don't notice our episodes of noncompliance, although we quickly spot them in others. It's the other guy who breaks a confidence, or litters, or texts while driving. Not us. We would never do that.

The takeaway: When we engage in noncompliance, we're not just being sloppy and lazy. It's more aggressive and rude than that. We're thumbing our noses at the world, announcing, "The rules don't apply to us. Don't rely on us. We don't care." We're drawing a line at good enough and refusing to budge beyond it.

Chapter 20

Becoming the Trigger

Remember Nadeem from Chapter 3, the London executive who allowed himself to be baited by his rival Simon? I promised to finish the story.

Nadeem dove into the change process with high motivation. He did all the things I asked of him. He got up in front of the eighteen people who participated in the 360-degree interviews and apologized for his behavior. He promised to do better. He asked everyone not to be shy about calling him out when he was backsliding into old behavior. He wanted their help. He also tried to build a positive relationship with Simon, although not without some reluctance at first. The old animus with Simon still exerted a pull on him.

"I'll meet Simon halfway," Nadeem told me. "He's got to change, too."

"Simon's not your responsibility," I said. "You only control how you behave."

"Why should I have to do all the work? If he doesn't make an effort, the hell with it."

"Go eighty percent of the way," I said. "See what happens."

Nadeem agreed and made it the top priority on his list of Daily Questions: *Did I try 80 percent with Simon?*

He started by apologizing to Simon, telling his alleged nemesis, "Whatever I've done in the past, I'm sorry. Our relationship has not worked, and I take responsibility for that. Starting today I'm going to do better." That's how change begins—with a commitment to improve and notifying people of your plan.

As Nadeem's coach, I checked in by phone on a regular basis for a progress report. Keep in mind that this took place while Nadeem was running a £20 billion division with 10,000 people in his charge. He had a family, he was traveling throughout the United Kingdom and Europe, he had corporate responsibilities and served on a few outside boards. He was a busy man. Keeping this top-of-mind was asking a lot. On the other hand, he also had his CEO and the head of human resources—the two people who hired me—closely monitoring his progress. Whatever the distractions of his day-to-day duties, he was highly motivated to solve his "Simon problem." He deeply believed that this was important for him as someone who wanted to be a company role model.

It didn't surprise me that Nadeem got better. All the structural motivators were in place, including regular follow-up. The surprise was how rapidly his Simon problem vanished. It happened in half a year. (Think about the deep grudges you have held against family, friends, and colleagues, the people you pass in silence in the hallway, can't forgive, refuse to talk to, or have deleted from your contact list. Would you be willing to repair that damage? Could you do it in six months? Or six years?)

It was such a success that Margot, the head of HR, asked Nadeem to talk about it to his direct reports and senior management. I wasn't there in London but Margot told me all about it.

On why it worked, Nadeem told the group, "I really reached out. I went out of my way to create a good relationship. More than Simon." Then he pulled out an email from Simon that he'd received that morning and read it aloud, as evidence of how the two men were on the same page now. "Practically reading each other's minds," he said.

Someone in the room asked, "What would you do differently?"

"I wouldn't go eighty percent of the way," Nadeem said. "I'd go a hundred percent. I learned that if I change my behavior, I change the people around me. If I'd gone all in, we'd have been friends even sooner."

There wasn't a dry eye in the room, I'm told.

This is the ultimate blessing of not settling for good enough. When we dive all the way into adult behavioral change—with 100 percent focus and energy—we become an irresistible force rather than the proverbial immovable object. We begin to change our environment rather than be changed by it. The people around us sense this. We have become the trigger.

Part Four

No Regrets

Chapter 21

The Circle of Engagement

What is the most memorable behavioral change you've made in your adult life?

I've posed this question to hundreds of people—and rarely does the answer come trippingly to their tongues.

The quickest responses come from people who've eliminated a bad habit. When I posed the question to Amy, a fifty-one-year-old senior executive at a media company, she immediately took credit for quitting smoking.

"That's not quite what I'm looking for," I said. "Kicking cigarettes is admirable and hard. But smoking is also unhealthy and socially disdained. There's a lot of external pressure to quit. I'm looking for voluntary behavioral change that made *other* people's lives better because you were better."

Amy thought about it. "Does being nicer to my mother count?"

That was more like it. Amy described a close mother-daughter relationship, perhaps too close. Her mother was in her late seventies and they spoke daily, but the conversation was governed by sniping and petty arguments. Parent and child were each engaged in a zero-sum game of proving herself right and the other wrong. "Love by a thousand cuts," Amy called it. One day, triggered by her mother's mortality and the realization that neither of them was getting younger, Amy decided on a truce. She didn't tell her mother about it. She simply refused to engage in the verbal skirmishing. When her mother made a judgmental remark Amy let it hang in the air like a noxious cloud, waiting for it to vaporize from neglect. With her daughter unwilling to counterpunch, Mom soon stopped punching. And vice versa.

"What you did is not minor," I said, congratulating Amy on an accomplishment more notable than quitting smoking. I asked her to imagine all the family holidays and Thanksgiving dinners and birthday parties and road trips that would be less fractious if people did as she did—declared a truce with their loved ones. "You changed the script for two people, not just yourself. That's something to be proud of."

Some people misunderstand the question. They recall a major career decision or an epiphany and confuse it with behavioral change. A financial executive cited his first year in law school when he knew that, unlike his father and brothers, he didn't want to be a lawyer. That was a moment of clarity that triggered everything that followed—quitting law school, becoming a financial analyst—but it was a fork in the road, not a behavioral change. Likewise, the art dealer who, with a straight face, described the moment he "realized that not everyone comes at a problem with my point of view." That's an insight (and not all that unique) but unless it profoundly changed how he treated other people, that's all it would have been—an insight.

A healthy number of people tell me about their triumphs of physical discipline and mental rigor: running a marathon, bench-pressing three hundred pounds, going back to school for an advanced degree, mastering bread making, learning to meditate. Again, commendable examples of self-improvement and not easily dismissed, but unless bread making or meditating has noticeably improved your behavior around others (as opposed to calming you down like taking a Valium), it's not the interpersonal achievement I'm hoping to hear. You've adopted a worthwhile activity, not changed your behavior.

The majority of people are stumped. They can't remember changing anything. (Quick question: what's the most memorable behavioral change *you* have made?)

Their blank stares don't surprise me. I get the same from most of my one-on-one clients in our first meeting. No matter how self-aware or alert to their surroundings these successful people may be, the need for behavioral change is not on their radar until I confront them with the evidence. We can't change until we know what to change.

We commit a lot of unforced errors in figuring out what to change.

We waste time on issues we don't feel that strongly about. We think, "It would be nice if I called my mother." But if it really mattered to us, we would do it, instead of mulling it over, making the occasional call, but never committing in a way that's satisfying and meaningful. We *wish* instead of *do*.

We limit ourselves with rigid binary thinking. Nadeem, for example, thought he had only two behavioral options in dealing with Simon: either grin and bear it (which was humiliating) or fight back (which only proved the folk wisdom, "Never wrestle with a pig—because you both get dirty but the pig loves it"). Nadeem didn't appreciate that his environment—any environment—is supple. It offers more than either/or. He had to be shown that his awkward situation was an opportunity to model positive behavior that would burnish his image as a team player and, as an unexpected bonus, help Simon become a better team player.

Mostly, we suffer a failure of imagination. Until a few years ago, I had never coached an executive who was also a medical doctor. I've now had the privilege of coaching three: Dr. Jim Yong Kim, the president of the World Bank; Dr. John Noseworthy, the president of the Mayo Clinic; and Dr. Raj Shah, the administrator of the United States Agency for International Development. Along with being brilliant, they are three of the most dedicated, high-integrity people I have ever met.

Early in my coaching process with each doctor I went over the six Engaging Questions:

1. Did I do my best to set clear goals?
2. Did I do my best to make progress toward my goals?
3. Did I do my best to find meaning?
4. Did I do my best to be happy?
5. Did I do my best to build positive relationships?
6. Did I do my best to be fully engaged?

These were smart, heavily credentialed men who are not generally thrown by simple questions. But I could see a confused look and then silence as each man considered the fourth question: *Did I do my best to be happy?*

"Do you have a problem with being happy?" I asked.

In three separate interactions, each man responded with

almost the same words: "It never occurred to me to try to be happy."

All three had the intellectual bandwidth to graduate from medical school and ascend to chief executive roles, and yet they had to be reminded to be happy. That's how difficult it is to know what we want to change. Even the sharpshooters among us can miss a really big target.

I can't tell you what to change. It's a personal choice. I could run through a list of gaudy qualities such as compassion, loyalty, courage, respect, integrity, patience, generosity, humility, etc. They are the timeless virtues that our parents, teachers, and coaches try to inculcate in us when we're young and malleable. We're frequently reminded of them in sermons, eulogies, and commencement addresses.

Being lectured on such virtues doesn't compel us to be virtuous. A speech, no matter how pointed or eloquently delivered, rarely triggers lasting change—not if we lack a compelling reason to change. We listen, nod our heads in agreement, then go back to our old ways. A big part of it is that we lack the structure to execute our ambitions; we are visionary Planners but blurry-eyed Doers. But as with the three doctors, it's also possible that some types of change never enter our minds.

That's a big reason I introduce clients to the Engaging Questions early on. I'm forcing people to consider questions so basic we often forget to ask them. I couple these six questions with my trademark tutorial about the environment—how we don't appreciate the good and (mostly) bad ways it shapes our behavior. And then I sit back and wait for the clients' cranial wheels to start turning. In my experience, forcing people to think about their environment in the context of fundamental desires like happiness, purpose, and engagement concentrates the mind, makes people reflect on how they're measuring up in those areas—and why.

When we assess our performance against the Engaging Questions and come up wanting in any way, we can lay the blame on either the environment or ourselves.

We love to scapegoat our environment. We don't set clear goals because we answer to too many people. We falter on existing goals because we have too much on our plate. We're unhappy because our job is a dead end. We don't form positive relationships because other people won't meet us halfway. We're disengaged at work because the company refuses to help us. And so on.

As skilled as we are at scapegoating our environment, we are equally masterful at granting ourselves absolution for any shortcomings. We rarely blame ourselves for mistakes or bad choices when the environment is such a convenient fall guy. How often have you heard a colleague accept responsibility for whatever misery he's feeling at work by admitting, "I'm a naturally miserable fellow"? The fault is out there somewhere, never within us.

Honestly assessing the interplay in our lives between these two forces—the environment and ourselves—is how we become the person we want to be.

My main goal in writing this book has been relatively modest: to help you achieve lasting positive change in the behavior that is most important to you. It's not my job to tell you what to change. With time to reflect, most of us know what we should be doing. My job is to help you do it. The change doesn't have to be enormous, the kind where people don't recognize you anymore. Any positive change is better than none at all. If as a result of some insight gained here, you're a little happier as you go through your day, or you have a slightly better relationship with the people you love, or you reach one of your goals, that's enough for me.

But I've also tried to highlight the value of two other objectives. They don't quite fit into the mold of the classic traditional virtues that our parents taught us. They're more like positive states of being.

The first objective is awareness—being awake to what's going on around us. Few of us go through our day being more than fractionally aware. We turn off our brains when we travel or commute to work. Our minds wander in meetings. Even among the people we love, we distract ourselves in front of a TV or computer screen. Who knows what we're missing when we're not paying attention?

The second is engagement. We're not only awake in our environment, we're actively participating in it—and the people who matter to us recognize our engagement. In most contexts, engagement is the most admirable state of being. It's both noble and pleasant, something we can be proud of and enjoy. Is there higher praise coming from a partner or child than to hear them tell us, "You are always there for me"? Or anything more painful than to be told, "You were never there for me"? That's how much engagement matters to us. It is the finest end product of adult behavioral change.

When we embrace a desire for awareness and engagement, we are in the best position to appreciate all the triggers the environment throws at us. We might not know what to expect—the triggering power of our environment is a constant surprise—but we know what others expect of us. And we know what we expect of ourselves. The results can be astonishing. We no longer have to treat our environment as if it's a train rushing toward us while we stand helplessly on the track waiting for impact. The interplay between us and our environment becomes reciprocal, a give-and-take arrangement where we are creating it as much as it creates us. We achieve an equilibrium I like to describe as the Circle of Engagement:

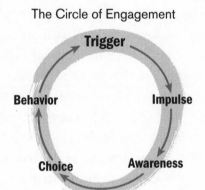

The Circle of Engagement

This is an easily achieved state of equilibrium. Let me give you an example of how it works using an everyday event so common (but not trivial) we barely take notice (but should). The story came to me in an email from an executive named Jim who had been in one of my Graduate Executive classes at Dartmouth's Tuck School of Business.

Jim's wife, Barbara, called him at work when he was having one of those Category 4 hurricane kind of days. Everything going wrong: clients ticked-off, division chief riding him, assistant called in sick. His wife said, "I just need someone to talk to." Evidently she was having a rough day at her job, too.

The statement *I just need someone to talk to* is a trigger—a trigger for Jim to stop what he's doing and *listen*. He's not being asked for his opinion or help. He's not being asked to say anything at all. Just listen. It is the easiest "ask" of his day. He should cherish it as an unexpected gift.

But at the precise moment Jim hears Barbara's voice, it's not a certainty that he will accept the call as a blessing. A trigger, after all, leads directly to an impulse to behave in a specific way, and Jim had a full menu of impulses to choose from, not all of them desirable.

He could become even more frazzled than he was before the phone rang. In other words, use the trigger to elevate his existing emotions.

He could tell his wife that he's really swamped at the moment and promise to call her back later or discuss it at home. In other words, delay the triggering moment for a time that's more convenient for him.

He could give Barbara his perfunctory attention and multitask while she's talking. In other words, award the trigger a lower priority than his wife attaches to it—and hope she doesn't notice.

He could have self-righteous thoughts about how his wife's problems pale in both severity and significance to his own and then demonstrate in exquisite detail that she is not as miserable as he is. In other words, he could compete with Barbara's trigger and "win." He could pursue the highly dubious strategy of proving that, once again, he is right and she is wrong.

Or he could listen.

These are all natural impulses. Who among us hasn't felt grumpy or lapsed into a full-blown tantrum while being forced to listen to someone else complain? Or tuned out a friend's whining by mentally traveling to another place? Or used another person's complaining as an occasion to broadcast and glorify our own travails?

When we lack awareness (in many cases because we are lost in what we're doing or feeling), we are easily triggered. The gap from trigger to impulse to behavior is instantaneous. That's the sequence. A trigger leads to an impulse, which leads directly to a behavior, which creates another trigger—and so on. Sometimes it works out for us; we're lucky and made the right "choice" without actually choosing. But it's an unnecessary risk that can produce chaos. Awareness is a difference maker. It stretches that triggering sequence, providing us with a little breathing space—not much, just enough—to consider our options and make a better behavioral choice.

Jim wrote the email to let me know he made the right choice. Here's his description of his first impulse at the triggering moment:

I was getting ready to point out that she wasn't the only person having problems. Then I remembered your words in class: "Am I willing at this time to make the investment required to make a positive contribution on this topic?" I took a breath and decided to be the guy who she needed to talk to. I didn't say a thing. When she finished venting, she said, "That felt good." All I could say was, "I love you."

This is the reciprocal miracle that appears when we are aware and engaged. We recognize a trigger for what it really is and respond wisely and appropriately. Our behavior creates a trigger that itself generates more appropriate behavior from the other person. And so on. This is what Jim accomplished with his wife's trigger. She triggered something thoughtful and wonderful in him, and he reciprocated by triggering a feel-good response in her. In the most positive way, each had become the other's trigger. Whether they knew it or not, they were running laps in a virtuous circle of engagement—and keeping the circle unbroken.

Chapter 22

The Hazard of Leading
a Changeless Life

Imagine living a life in which nothing changed.

I'm not talking about working at the same company your entire adult life, or staying married to the same person for fifty years, or never leaving the community you were born in. Those are choices to be honored, not regretted or derided. At the far side of a long and happy existence, they reflect a sturdy permanence worth celebrating.

Nor am I talking about going through life and never changing the food we order in a restaurant, the style of clothes we wear, the music and TV shows and books we enjoy, even the social and political views we hold. Going through life and *never* changing our tastes, opinions, and everyday preferences, even if we're the most obdurate person in the world, is unimaginable—because our environment won't allow it. The world around us changes and we change with it, if only because it's easier to go with the flow.

Even among the steadiest of people—the kind living in the

same house with the same partner and working at the same job their entire adult life—it's hard to imagine a completely changeless existence.

And yet there's one aspect of our lives where we wear changelessness as a badge of honor. I'm talking about our interpersonal behavior and our resistance to changing how we treat other people.

The sister we haven't seen or spoken to in years because of some long-forgotten grievance.

The old friend we still tease with a cruel childhood nickname that he's long outgrown.

The neighbor we've seen for years and, out of shyness or inertia or indifference, have never introduced ourselves to.

The customers we resent for the demands they place on us.

The anger we display that is so inevitable our family members take bets on when we will erupt.

The scolding response when a child disappoints us.

Most of us would mock a restaurant that never changed its menu. But we are not so reproachful or mocking with ourselves. We take a foolish pride in prolonging some behaviors as long as possible, with no regard for who is harmed. Only when it's too late to undo the damage and we have reached some objective distance do we rethink our behavior, perhaps regret it. Why did we go all those years without talking to our sister? Why were we cruel to our best friend? What relationship did we miss by not introducing ourselves to a neighbor? Why not thank a customer for placing the order? What would it cost us to offer a soothing word to our upset child?

When we prolong negative behavior—both the kind that hurts the people we love or the kind that hurts us in some way—we are leading a changeless life in the most hazardous manner. We are willfully choosing to be miserable and making others miserable, too. The time we are miserable is time we can never get back. Even more painful, it was all our doing. It was our choice.

In this book's opening pages, I promised that if I did my job properly, you the reader would have a little less regret in your life.

Now it's your turn. I'm not asking much. As you close this book, think about one change, one triggering gesture, that you won't regret later on. That's the only criterion: you won't feel sorry you did it. Maybe it's calling your mother to tell her you love her. Or thanking a customer for his loyalty. Or saying nothing instead of something cynical in a meeting. It could be anything, as long as it represents a departure, however modest, from what you've always done and would continue doing forever.

Then do it.

It will be good for your friends. It will be good for your company. It will be good for your customers. It will be good for your family.

And even better for you. So much better, you will want to do it again.

Acknowledgments

I would like to thank my coaching clients, who are among the most fantastic leaders in the world. I have learned far more from them than they have learned from me. I would particularly like to thank Frances Hesselbein and Alan Mulally, who are two of the greatest leaders who have ever lived and who have been helping me for over two decades.

I would like to thank my friends at Profile Books, who have been wonderful partners and supporters.

Figures in **bold** type refer to diagrams, those in *italics* to photographs.

7-Eleven convenience stores 13

A

ABC (antecedent, behavior, and consequence) sequencing template 54–5, **55**

ability 5, 6, 62, 64, 85

motivation and understanding 5, 6

accountability 103, 141

active questions 101–110, 113

employee engagement 104–8

follow-up after training 108, 109, 110

and goals 117

passive questions 102–3, 109–110

putting active questions to the test 108–110

role of 114

added value 144–5, 179, 180

admiration 48–9

air travel 26, 105–6

AIWATT 152–66, 210

circumstances for deploying AIWATT 159–65

when decisions don't go our way 164–5

when our facts collide with other people's beliefs 162–3

when we confuse disclosure with honesty 159–61

when we have an opinion 161–2

when we regret our own decisions 165

create false positives 156–8

a delaying mechanism 158

it's always an empty boat 153–5, 157–8

role of 166

text discussed 158–9

Alicia's story (HR head) 94–5

Amabile, Teresa: *The Progress Principle* 112

ambition xv, 104–5, 143, 225

American Red Cross 150

Amy's story (media company executive) 221–2

anger xv, xvii, 46, 50, 61, 74, 119, 134, 147, 150, 154, 155, 165, 189, 211, 215, 233

antecedent (in ABC sequence) 54, **55**, 56, 57

apathy 50

apology 36, 101, 186, 202, 216, 217

asking for help 101, 121, 125, 126, 135

assertiveness 51

Associated Press 149

Austen, Jane: *Pride and Prejudice* xvi–xvii

authentic self, loss of 23–4

authority
at home 79
at work 34

awareness 44, 45, 46, 56, 57, 59, 66, 72, 83, 191, 198, 201, 227, 230

B

"backfire effect" 163

baldness, accepting 6–7

Baumeister, Roy F. 182

"bedtime procrastination" 33

behavior (in ABC sequence) 54, **55**, 57

behavioral change, immutable truths of 3–11
duration of desire for change 4

major/minor 4
previously successful 4–5
Truth#1 Meaningful behavioral change is very hard to do 4–7
Truth#2 No one can make us change unless we truly want to change 7–10

Beijing Olympics 205

belief triggers 5, 12–24
"at least I'm better than ..." 17
an epiphany will suddenly change my life 20
I have all the time in the world 18–19
I have the wisdom to assess my own behavior 24
I have willpower and won't give in to temptation 15–16
I shouldn't need help and structure 17–18
I won't get distracted and nothing unexpected will occur 19–20
I won't get tired and my enthusiasm will not fade 18
if I change I am "inauthentic" 23–4
if I understand, I will do 14–15
Mayor Bloomberg's "social engineering" 12–13

my change will be permanent
    and I will never have to
    worry again 20–21
my efforts will be fairly
    rewarded 22–3
my elimination of old
    problems will not bring on
    new problems 21–2
no one is paying attention to
    me 23
today is a special day 16
blame 31–2, 103, 116, 117, 119,
    154, 160–61, 174, 215, 226
Blanchard, Ken 62, 63
blogging 121, 162
Bloomberg, Michael 12–13
body language 34
boredom 56, 87, 91, 107
BPR *see* Business Plan Review
brainwashing 21
Business Plan Review (BPR)
    developed by Mulally 169–
        70
    executives' changing attitude
        to 172–3
    resistance to 171–2
    rules of 170, 187
    structure of 170–71, 187

C
career changes 4
casino environment 32
CEOs
    achieving dream job 21–2

first meeting with 59
    problems of being CEO 22
    retirement 143–4
    unprepared for corporate exit
        87–8
    and the wheel of change
        87–8, 92
"change profile" 125–6, 128
changelessness
    celebrating permanence 232
    environmental changes 232
    in interpersonal relationships
        233–4
checklists, aversion to 17, 172
children
    childhood obesity 12
    different responses to triggers
        47
    losing temper with 57
    problem behavior 54
    time spent with 51
choices 53
    careless 183
    commodifying 203
    considered 57–8, 59, 61,
        201, 230
    deferred choices xvii
    environment blamed for bad
        choices 226
    and fate xvi
    foolish 182
    inevitable negative choices
        97–8
    lack of 187

long-term 232
low depletion 186
low willpower 187
random 203
and structure 187
voluntary activity 209
circle of engagement 221–31,
228
awareness and engagement
227–31
the Engaging Questions
224–6
most memorable behavioral
change 221–3
unforced errors in figuring
out what to change 223–4
clients' stakeholders 3–4
coaching 140–51
benefits of Daily Questions
eventually we become our
own Coach 148–51, *149*
if we do it, we get better
147–8
we get better faster 147–8
a follow-up mechanism 141
Griffin's story 144–7
instills accountability 141
leader as coach 142–3
and planner/doer dynamic
141–2, **141**
resistance to 143
scorekeeper, referee, adviser
140
sports 142

Cold War arms race 43
comfort zone 5
commitment 21, 114, 139, 198,
209, 217
devices 135–6
commuting 96, 97
"competing response" 56
competitiveness xv, 25
complaining 157, 164, 165,
229–30
complexity 17, 56, 173
compliance issues 213–15
compliments 49, 93, 212
confidence 6, 64, 122, 127
and delegation 64
and environment changes
34
increased 42
lack of 63–4
overconfidence 16, 24
at start of day 66
confirmation bias 162–3
confusion 15
consequence (in ABC
sequence) 54, **55**, 56, 57
control
and the environment xvi,
26–7, 32
and good behavior 43
and other people's
unpredictability 10
sense of 114
sleep needs 32
see also self-control

counterproductive behavior, examples of 93–4, 156–7
creativity 104, 113, 145
crises 19–20, 70
2008 financial crisis 111
cue (in habit loop) 55, 56
customer feedback 93
cynicism 28, 50, 107, 108, 158, 193, 234

D

Daily Questions 115–20, **118**, 172, 174, 188, 191, 199
adapting into Hourly Questions 195, 196
Daily Questions in action 124–39
Emily's story 124–34, 135
creating 133–4, **133**
eliminating scores 129–32, **129**, **131**
she asked for help 126
she had no track record of success 127–8
she was going solo 126
she was in a "hostile" environment 126–7
six goals 128
they highlight the difference between self-discipline and self-control 137–8
they ignite our motivation where we need it 136–7

they reinforce our commitment 135–6
they shrink our goals into manageable increments 138–9
deadlines 39, 70–71, 190
decision fatigue 183
decision-making 164, 165, 183, 186
delegation 67, 96, 105
denial 9, 14, 84, 143
Dennis's story (C-level executive) 210–212
depletion 18
Derek's story (dealing with grief) 190–91
diet xv–xvi, 5, 116–17, 119, 121
see also weight gain/loss
discipline xv, 16, 17, 21, 33, 121, 196
Hourly Questions 199
and initial enthusiasm 130
lack of 26, 182, 200
quirky 50
and quitting smoking 9–10
self-regulated 115
and structure 187, 188
disrespect 8, 49
distractions 19–20, 26, 49, 51
doctor-patient relationship 213–14
"dramatic narrative fallacy" 78n
driver feedback 40–42

Drucker, Peter 76, 91, 153, 156, 157, 164

Duhigg, Charles
Golden Rule of Habit Change 55
habit loop 55–6
The Power of Habit 55

E
effort
and depletion 18
failing to make an effort xiii, xvii
focus on 129
hierarchy of 122
and inertia 5
in making marriage proposal 74
measuring 114, 117, 130
redundant 68
rewards for 22–3, 139, 146–7
to accept people's foibles 28
ego depletion 181–8
behavior under its influence 184–5
codifying depleting events 185–6
and consumer behavior 183–4
decision-making 183, 186
and an enjoyable evening event 200
example of 181–2
and interpersonal behavior 184, 189
an invisible enemy 184
overcoming it with structure 187–8
and self-control 182–3, 185
ego strength 182, 185
emails
checking 51
harassing xviii
Emily's story (weight loss) 124–34, 135
employees
coaching 63
delegating to 64
directing 63
engagement 102, 104–8, 114
excuses for being late for work 14
and extrinsic motivation 137
follow-up 108, 109, 110
performance readiness 62–3
recruitment 95
supporting 63–4
training 102, 105, 108, 109, 110
and wheel of change 94–6
energy 18, 67, 90, 158, 188, 205, 218
engagement 58, 78, 81, 102, 104–110, 152, 227
four levels of 106–8, **107**
committed 106–7
cynical 107

hostile 107–8
professional 107
full 114
in meetings 192, 193
engaging questions 111–23,
224–6
   Daily Questions 115–20, **118**
   Did I do my best to be fully
     engaged today? 114
   Did I do my best to be happy
     today? 113, 224–5
   Did I do my best to build
     positive relationships
     today? 113
   Did I do my best to find
     meaning today? 112–13
   Did I do my best to make
     progress towards my goals
     today? 112
   Did I do my best to set clear
     goals today? 111–12
   a distinction with a difference
     120–23
   improvement seen on follow
     up 114
enthusiasm 1, 18, 82, 106, 130,
206
entitlement 25–6
environment 25–38
   alters throughout the day
     33
   appreciation of 6
   behavior shaped by 5–6,
     25–6, 27–8, 225

   belief that in control of
     environment 35–6
   changed by one factor 28–9
   control by 26–7, 38
   control of 134, 173
   cool 29
   creating 75
   fate and choice xvi
   feedback from 43–4, 84–5
   home 79, 80
   hostile 25, 27, 67, 126–7,
     146
   learning 105
   mindfulness about 51
   overspending in shopping
     malls 31–2
   "planner" and "doer"
     responses 85
   power of 26, 31, 73, 185,
     227
   sales 31
   scapegoating 226
   situational 34–7, 39
   sleep 32–3
   state of equilibrium 228
   triggering undesirable
     behavior xv-xvi, 84, 98,
     143, 158
   ugly 50
   unethical 29–30
   see also forecasting the
     environment
epiphanies 20
exceptionalism 18

excuses 5, 14, 16, 17, 24, 49,
  84, 119, 142, 208
exercise 14, 128, 130
  see also getting into shape
expectations
  of crises 20
  falling short of 14
  low 106
  and resentment 22
  unrealistic 19

F
Facebook 51, 162
family
  consequences of impulsive
    behavior 60–61
  and depletion 186–7
  settling for good enough
    211–12
  time spent with 97
  and work commitments xvi
fate xvi
fatigue 50, 183
fear 49
feedback
  360-degree 8, 30, 176, 180
  customer 93
  driver 40–42
  from clients' stakeholders 3
  from colleagues 39–40,
    178
  from leaders 105
  and good performance
    205–6

feedback loop 41–4, 205
  action 42, 43
  consequence 42, 43
  and the environment 43–4
  evidence 42, 43
  relevance 42, 43
  triggering desirable behavior
    44
financial crisis (2008) 111
follow-up 17, 108–111, 115,
  128, 129, 141, 214n, 217
Ford Motor Company 169,
  170, 171, 173, 175, 187
forecasting the environment
  73–83
  adjustment 73, 81–3, 85
  anticipation 73, 74–6, 85
  avoidance 73, 76–81, 85
  weather 73
forgiveness 101, 202
Fortune magazine 89, 169
Francis, Pope 169
Frankl, Viktor: *Man's Search
  for Meaning* 112
Freedom program 135
frustration xvii, 119, 194
future challenges,
  misunderstanding of 22

G
Gallup research 105, 113
Gawande, Dr. Atul 122–3
  The Checklist Manifesto 17,
    122

getting into shape 7, 21, 51, 142, 143
see also exercise; weight loss
Gilbert, Daniel: *Stumbling on Happiness* 113
Girl Scouts of America 89–90
goals
achieving 21, 49
and active questions 117
behavioral 49, 51
blocked by the environment 44, 50
clear 102–3, 111, 112
and delegation 67
happiness 20–21
health and fitness 121
listing 136
long-term 49
maintaining 21
marginal 207
personal 71
setting xv, 18, 21, 103, 176, 178
time management 121
Goldsmith, Kelly 67–8, 102, 103, 108, 109, 116
Goldsmith, Lyda 6, 28, 52, 68, 115–16, 117
Goldsmith, Marshall: *What Got You Here Won't Get You There* 144–5n
golf 78n, 96, 97, 206
"good enough" 202–215
environments triggering

"good enough" behavior 204–215
when our motivation is marginal 204–8
when we behave like "amateurs" 210–213
when we have compliance issues 213–15
when we're working pro bono 208–210
Nadeem's not settling for "good enough" 216–18
"satisficing" 203
setting the bar too low 204
settling for 203–4, 206–7
gratitude 59, 118–19, 150
Great Western Disease 20
grief 190–91
Griffin's story (adding too much value at work) 144–7, 195–7
guidance 18, 63, 67, 68, 69, 153

H
habit loop 55–6
Hackman, Gene 64n
hairstyle changes 4, 159
happiness 20–21, 45, 109, 110, 113, 115, 116, 224–5
Hersey, Paul 62, 63, 90, 91
Hesselbein, Frances 89–90, 208
Holt, Lester 58–9

Homer: *The Odyssey* 15–16
honesty 172, 178, 226
  vs disclosure 159–61
Hoosiers (film) 64*n*
hopelessness 50
hostility 107–8
Hourly Questions 194–201
  adapted from Daily
    Questions 195, 196
  awareness 198
  commitment 198
  the dreaded event 199
  and an enjoyable evening
    event 200–201
  people 199–200
  pre-awareness 197–8
  repetition 198
  scoring 198
  self-testing 194, 201
  short-term utility 199
  structure 196, 197, 198
human resources (HR) 94, 104
humility 18
hybrid cars 12, 43
hypocrisy 13, 210

I
"I told you so" 156, 157
imagination 224
immunity, false sense of 17
impatience xviii, 25, 138–9,
  194
impulses 16, 20, 230
  competing 17–18

consequences of impulsive
    behavior within family
    60–61
  and an epiphany 20
  stifling 57, 60
  yielding to first impulse
    57–8, 60
inconsistency 16
inertia 5, 7, 33, 77, 88, 158,
  233
insight 20, 222
integrity 34, 97, 208, 209,
  224, 225
intellectual stimulation 121
isolation 23, 50

J
Jim's story (response to wife's
  trigger) 228–31
job changes 4
Johnson, Samuel 76

K
Kennedy, John F. 109
Kim, Dr. Jim Yong 164–5, 224
Kübler-Ross's five stages of
  grief 191

L
Late Show (TV show) 29*n*
leadership
  behavior altered to suit
    environment 35
  feedback from leaders 105

and power 78
see also situational leadership
"Leadership Is a Contact
  Sport" research 21
Letterman, David 29*n*
"letting go" 132, 152
Liebling, A.J. 161
listening 3, 7, 30, 65, 115, 126,
  127, 172, 225, 229
long-term benefit 47, 48
Lose It! app 135
loss aversion 50
lottery winners 22
loved ones
  and changing behavior 10
  failing to spend time with xvi
  grief at passing 190–91
  hurting xix
  truce with 222
low-probability events 19, 61,
  67

M
magic moves 101, 121
magical thinking 20
Mali 149–51
market share 93
marriage 74
Mayo Clinic 224
meaning 109, 110, 112–13, 115,
  116, 192
medication
  "medicine adherence" apps
    214*n*

pillbox 187–8
meetings
  committing to being
    miserable in a dull meeting
    191, 194
  first meeting with CEO 59
  post-meeting testing 192–3,
    194–5
  and professional poise 211
  staff 69–70
  and structure 191–3
  see also Business Plan Review
Merkel, Angela 169
metrics 93
mindfulness 37, 57, 58, 198
misery 50, 106, 187, 191, 193,
  194, 226, 229, 234
"mom and pop" stores 13
moods, and weather 45–6
moral superiority 156–7
motivation 17, 139
  and delegation 64
  extrinsic 136–7
  flagging 67
  and goals 49
  and "good enough" behavior
    194–8
  intrinsic 136, 137
  levels of 62
  and quitting smoking 9–10
  and regret xix
  and reward 23
  sleep needs 32
  at start of day 66

understanding and ability 5, 6
Mulally, Alan 127, 169–73, 175, 177, 179, 187

N
Nadeem's story ("Simon problem") 36–8, 39–40, 42–3, 98, 216–18, 223–4
nail-biting habit 55–6, 57, 121
"nanny state" 13
National Association for the Advancement of Colored People (NAACP) 13
NBC News 150
need-to-win syndrome 213
Netflix 49
New Year's resolutions 207
New York 13, 195–6
Noseworthy, Dr. John 224
not-invented-here syndrome 213

O
objectivity 24
office door, closing 13, 166
online shopping sites 32
optimism 101, 160
ostracism 49, 50
other people
  and anticipated triggers 46
  blamed 24, 226
  considering 56–7
  disappointing 14, 186
  and extrinsic motivation 136
  and "false positives" 156
  and goals 128, 144, 148
  and "magical moves" 101
  making their lives better 221
  managing 174
  participation in new behavior 126
  relying on 10
  resistance to changing treatment of 233
  rules of 182
  self-assessment 24
  tempting you away from objectives 67
  their need for change 17
  upsetting 186
overconfidence 16, 24

P
pain
  as a discouraging trigger 50
  and regret xviii, 31
  a trigger for change xix
parenting 47, 51
passive questions 102–3, 109–10, 116
passivity 78, 106, 107, 116, 185
patience xvii, xviii, 51, 139
paying attention 58, 59
Peck, Gregory 64n
pedantry 156
peer pressure xv, 50–51
performance readiness levels 62–3

performance reviews 211
permanence 232
  false sense of 21
pessimism 199
Phelps, Michael 205
Phil's story xiii-xiv, xv, xvi, 46
photosynthesis 43
positive change 4, 5, 20, 21,
  226
positive difference 109, 153,
  156, 159, 166
power
  of the environment 26, 31,
    73, 185, 227
  of inertia 5
  of leaders 78
  of triggers to lead astray 15
praise xv, 48–9, 91, 178, 227
pre-awareness 197–8
pre-mindfulness 198
privacy 143
pro bono work 137, 208–9
procrastination 19
punctuality 202

Q
quality scores 93
questions see active questions;
  engaging questions; passive
  questions

R
racism, perceived 36–7
radar speed displays (RSDs) 41

recognition 23, 48–9, 105, 137
regression 4, 21
regret xvi–xix, 234
  deferred choices xvii
  failure to change unwanted
    behavior xvi
  lack of effort xvii
  lack of respect for xviii
  negative behavior 233
  opportunities squandered xvii
  pain associated with xviii-xix
  replaying actions xviii
  undeveloped talents xvii
reinforcement 46, 61, 72, 135,
  205
  positive 49, 52
relationships
  doctor-patient 213–14
  with the environment 84
  family 61, 121
  interpersonal 93, 105
  leader/follower 63, 65
  mother-daughter 221–2
  positive 109, 110, 113, 192,
    216, 224, 226
  and resistance to change 9
  and temptation 77
  trigger festivals and
    consequences 60–61
Rennie's story 68–70, 98
reputation 126
  damage to 29–30
  Nadeem's story 36, 42
  poor xvii

win-at-all-costs 210

resentment 22, 24, 165
  racial 37

resistance to change
  beliefs triggering 5, 14, 84
  excuses 5
  lack of awareness that
    change is desirable 5
  lack of commitment 8–9

respect 10
  of colleagues 36, 37, 42
  at home 34

responsibility 3, 53, 79, 94,
  103, 109, 113, 114, 117, 158,
  172, 179, 193, 214n, 216,
  217, 226

restaurants 25–6

reward 22–3, 48–9, 136
  in habit loop 55, 56

Richard's story 213–14

"road rage" 25

Robert's story see structure
  fitting the situation

rote repetition 98

routine (in habit loop) 55, 56

rules 49

S
Sachi's story 81–3
San Diego 73
sarcasm 28, 36–7, 50
"satisficing" 203
Schubert, Richard 148
self-assessment 24, 67

self-awareness 188, 199, 223

self-control 15, 18, 126, 137,
  138, 139, 182–3, 185, 187,
  196

self-delusion 14

self-discipline 67, 137, 138,
  139, 188

self-exemption 17

self-improvement 143, 223
  ambitions 143
  civic 12
  classic menu 128
  goals 18
  projects 122

self-indulgence 16

self-management 67, 68

self-monitoring 5, 98, 134

self-regulation 182, 183, 185

self-respect 126

self-scoring 141, 172, 191, 198

self-sufficiency 144

self-testing 194, 196, 201

Selye, Hans 185

Shah, Dr. Raj 224

shopping malls 31–2

short-term gratification 16, 47,
  48, 49

Simon, Herbert 203

situational leadership 62–5
  coaching employees 63
  delegating to employees 64
  directing employees 63
  Hersey's and Blanchard's
    concept 62

and performance readiness of
followers 62–3
and self-managed adult
behavioral change 67, 69
supporting employees 63–4
sleep 32–3, 49, 115, 119
smoking 9–10, 12, 55, 57, 221,
222
social engineering 12
social media 135, 161
special days 16
spending while impaired (SWI)
186
staff meetings 69–70
Stan's story (family foundation)
78–80, 98
Steve's story (wheel of change
choices) 96–7
Stewart, Jon 13
stress 50, 60, 184, 185
structure
Business Plan Review 169–
73
Daily Questions 128
and ego depletion
187–8
and an enjoyable evening
event 200–201
examples of its use in daily
life 173–4
governing predictable parts
of our lives 189
Hourly Questions 196, 197,
198

importance in turning around
an organization 169
limits options 173
and meetings 191–3
the pillbox 187–8
seizing control of the
environment 173
simple repetition 172
simplifying complexity 173
surgeons' rejection of hand-
washing checklist 17, 172
therapeutic 190–91
structure fitting the situation
(Robert's story) 175–80
bi-monthly meeting format
177
meeting agenda
how can I become a more
effective leader? 179
how can I help? 178–9
what is going well? 178
where are we going? 177–8
where are you going? 178
where can we improve?
178
Robert's 360-degree
feedback 176, 180
team's involvement in
Robert's transformation
179
time saved 180
stubbornness 23
succeeding alone 17–18
success: defined 139

sugary soft drinks 12–13
superior planners, inferior
  doers 62–72
  both leader and follower
    65–7
  coaching clients unable to
    follow rules 71–2
  examples 70
  plans contradicted by
    previous actions 70–71
  Rennie's story 68–70
  situational leadership 62–5
sycophancy 210

T
targets 112, 121
temptation 77–8
time
  management 121
  warped view of 18–19
Today (TV programme) 58–9
tolerance 28, 210
training 102, 105, 108, 109,
  110
transparency 172
triggers
  anticipated 46
  belief *see* belief triggers
  conscious 45
  counterproductive xv, 47,
    49, 50
  defined xv, 44
  differing responses 47
  direct 44

discouraging 46, 49, 50, 52
encouraging 46, 47, 48, 49,
  52
external 45
how they work 54–61
and impulses 230
indirect 44–5
internal 45
and pain of regret xix
peer pressure 50–51
positive 229–31
potency of environmental
  triggers xvi-xvi
productive 47, 48, 50, 51
pulling and pushing us off
  course 10
resistance to change 5
types of xv
unconscious 45–6
unexpected xv, 46
we don't need it or want it 50
we need it but don't want it
  49–50
we want it but don't need it
  49
we want it and need it 28–9
we want it vs. we need it
  matrix 48–53, **48**
truths of behavioral change
  3–11
  clients' stakeholders 3–4
  meaningful behavioral
    change is very hard to do
    4–7

three problems 5–6
three questions 4–5
no one can make us change
unless we truly want to
change 7–11
trying 13, 84, 98, 114, 117, 121,
129, 139
TV 116, 182, 227
commercials 21
as a distraction 49
and sleep needs 33
time management 121
Twelve O'Clock High (film) 64n
Twitter 162
Tyson, Mike 72

U
understanding
motivation and ability 5, 6
sleep needs 32
United States Agency for
International Development
224
Utrecht University 33

V
victimhood 114, 151, 154
visibility 172
voluntary work 207–8

W
Warby Parker 135–6
weather, and mood 45–6
weddings 27, 67, 68, 74, 131,
205
weight gain/loss 5, 52–3,
55, 88, 115, 124–34, 135,
213–14
see also diet
wheel of change 84–100, 118
accepting 86, 92–5, 96, 119,
133
chart 85–6, **86**, 88
Change to Keep axis 85
Positive to Negative axis
85
creating 86, 87–8, 92, 95,
96, 118, 132, 133
eliminating 86, 90–91, 92,
94, 95–6, 119, 133
and employees 94–6
preserving 86, 89–90, 92,
95, 96, 118–19, 132–3
Whole Foods 124, 126
willpower 15, 16, 20, 77, 186,
187, 205
working out 51–2, 181
World Bank 164–5, 224